SECOND CHANCES

TRANSFORMING BITTERNESS TO HOPE AND THE STORY OF RUTH

SECOND CHANCES

TRANSFORMING BITTERNESS TO HOPE AND THE STORY OF RUTH

Rabbi Levi Meier, Ph.D.

URIM PUBLICATIONS
Jerusalem • New York

Second Chances: Transforming Bitterness to Hope
and the Story of Ruth
by Rabbi Levi Meier, Ph.D.

First Edition
ISBN 965-7108-67-5

Urim Publications, P.O. Box 52287, Jerusalem 91521 Israel
Lambda Publishers Inc.
3709 13th Avenue Brooklyn, New York 11218 U.S.A.
Tel: 718-972-5449 Fax: 718-972-6307
mh@ejudaica.com

www.UrimPublications.com

Dedicated

to

Uriela Obst Sagiv

who journeyed from

Poland to Los Angeles to Jerusalem

and has become a

Contemporary Ruth

CONTENTS

ACKNOWLEDGMENTS

It has been my privilege to serve as Rabbi to converts who have enriched the entire Jewish people. One of my best students has been Uriela Obst Sagiv, to whom this book is dedicated. I thank her for her inspiration and assistance, as she continues to learn Torah and live Torah in her new home in Jerusalem.

Sometimes, people born into a religion maintain a secret hierarchy, seeing themselves on one level and converts on a different level. This book dispels such a mistaken idea. Converts are on an even higher level than those who are born into the faith, having chosen this path.

I want to thank Paula Van Gelder for her great editorial assistance in the production of this book.

I also want to recognize those who have carefully read the manuscript and made valuable suggestions: Deena Brandes; Constance Courage; Rabbi Joseph Levine; my dear brother, Rabbi Menahem Meier, and my esteemed colleague, Dr. Fred Rosner.

INTRODUCTION

When people call or write to invite me to a wedding, they are quick to point out what a wonderful match their son or daughter has made. "He's such a wonderful young man," they say. "He's in his last year of dental school at an Ivy League university, and he's an all-around great guy. He's good-looking, athletic and has the most impeccable manners. A real *mensch*. And his parents are very well known in the community. They're philanthropic and they've even endowed a high school that is named in their honor. We couldn't be happier."

I rejoice at such wonderful news. The coming together of two people is truly a cause for celebration. However, many of us seem to focus on the socio-economic status of the bride and groom, their lineage and the esteem in which they are held by their peers. We do not give as much thought to the future home that these two unique individuals will build together.

Our reactions are understandable. However, I can't help thinking back to a marriage of a different sort, one which took place about three thousand years ago – that of Ruth and Boaz. I wonder how many people of today would have attended such a ceremony and what they might have said about the family background of the couple. After all, Ruth was a convert to Judaism from Moab, a nation born of incest and with a history of cruel insensitivity, particularly toward the Jews. Boaz was the descendent of a union that came about through sexual deception between Judah and his daughter-in-law, Tamar. This is not the sort of information that is usually included in announcements on the society pages of *The New York Times*.

Yet, the marriage of Ruth and Boaz was a holy, blessed and joyful occasion. Furthermore, the progeny produced by this couple's union are among the most noble in human history. Ruth and Boaz are the parents of Oved, who was the father of Jesse, the father of King David, from whose very line the Messiah, the ultimate hope for all humanity, is destined to come. This is why Ruth is called "Mother of Royalty."[1]

In order to better understand the origins of Ruth and Boaz, as well as their sacred missions in life, let us briefly review their stories, which are summarized in a note at the end of this book.[2] The details may be difficult to grasp in one reading, but that does not matter. The main point is that Ruth and Boaz, the heroes of our story, emanate from less than heroic beginnings, to say the least.

I venture to say that most parents today would not approve of a match with a Boaz or a Ruth. Yet their union, regardless of the history of their families, leads to greatness. How can the most sublime offspring originate from such beginnings? How can a nation honor these people as heroes and role models?

---

[1] Talmud, *Bava Batra* 91b

[2] See Appendix D.

To study the story of Ruth and Boaz is to walk back along shadowy family paths. We may be surprised by some of the details along the way, but when we examine this story carefully, we will find that it is essential to the understanding of just what greatness can emerge from a troubled past.

* * *

In this work, we will explore how Ruth and Boaz ultimately came to meet and to change the course of history and of humankind. Central to their story – and to ours – is the role of hope after tragedy. In so many stories of the Bible, as indeed in the universal stories that give us inspiration to cope with the chaotic state of the world, can be found the message that hope always endures. No matter what the circumstances, no matter how black the darkness, hope is always there. Sometimes it is buried in the bottom of a sea of muck; sometimes it is hidden in a chest of earthly treasures, the only priceless object there. But if we try, we can always find it and hold onto it.

I am writing this at the beginning of the 21st century, shortly after the confidence of America has been shaken as never before by seemingly unimaginable events. People have asked: Is hope still possible? How is dialogue possible when different cultures misunderstand one another to the extent that murder is considered not only permissible, but indeed a martyr's key to "paradise"?

And yet, the Bible tells us that God runs the world. We are living out His plan for humankind, and our free will gives us the ability to choose to be heroes or villains or bystanders in the eternal story of humanity. Hope gives us the strength to do what we must do based on faith in the future.

In this work, we will examine the Book of Ruth and mine it for lessons that speak to us today. We will explore ways of coping with human suffering and investigate why the Messiah emanates from an ancestry that includes incest and sexual deception. We will also try to understand the essential nature of man and woman, as well as their relationship to one another. This discussion will also shed light on the essence of human sensuality and sexuality.

In this process, we will compare and contrast the story of Ruth with stories from today – stories of despair and stories of courage drawn from my own experiences as a Jungian psychologist, teacher, hospital chaplain and rabbi, and from the lives of my clients, my patients and members of my Bible study groups. I trust that in this way we will find together, in this story, the bottomless reservoir of hope that is accessible to each of us.

Too often, we feel imprisoned by the past. So many of my clients and patients have shared with me tales of trauma and abuse as they attempt to understand the wounds and scars that they still bear. They seek ways to break out of old patterns and avoid repeating the mistakes of the past, even when these are the only models they know. The work they undertake is vitally important in their quest to live life as fully and meaningfully as possible.

Everyone has secrets, personal and familial. Sometimes these secrets feel overwhelming, dooming one generation to repeat the mistakes of parents and others from our pasts. However, for each of us, I offer a message of reassurance and hope found in the

Book of Ruth. Past interpersonal or family patterns need not determine our present or our future. We need not inevitably copy some of the poor behavior of parents or even more distant ancestors. Even the poor choices that family members made hundreds – or thousands! – of years ago, can be repaired and redeemed by what we decide to do today. We have the power to rectify the past.

This is a truly awesome gift. As we shall see from the story of Ruth, we each hold in our own hands the key that can unlock a world of blessings for ourselves, for those who came before us, and for those who will follow us.

Part I: HOPE

The Book of Ruth (Summary of Chapter 1)

There is a famine in the land of Bethlehem. A man named Elimelech takes his wife, Naomi, and their two sons, Machlon and Kilyon, and moves from Bethlehem, in Judah, to the land of Moab. There, Elimelech dies, and his sons marry gentile Moabite women, Ruth and Orpah. Some ten years later, Machlon and Kilyon also die, leaving no heirs. Naomi hears that Bethlehem is no longer afflicted by famine, so she sets out to return there, accompanied by her two daughters-in-law. However, she urges them to return to their own families, reminding them that they still have the opportunity to remarry. Orpah cries, and she eventually decides to stay in Moab, her homeland, and not to return with Naomi. However, nothing that Naomi says can dissuade Ruth, who remains by her mother-in-law's side. Naomi and Ruth return to Bethlehem and arrive at the beginning of the barley harvest. When they are met by the women of the city, Naomi tells the people of her losses and bitter life.

Chapter 1

FAMINE

The Book of Ruth begins on a somber note: *"And it happened in the days when the Judges judged that there was a famine in the land...."*[1]

Famine means great hunger. Famine means a time when there is nothing to eat and no produce is available. People put unimaginable things into their mouths in order to try to get some nourishment. Weak and tired, the hungry walk for miles in search of food and water, their bodies growing thinner, their children turning into small skeletons with distended bellies. When things get bad enough, people succumb to a variety of diseases that plague the malnourished. Many die, while others hover between life and death, desperately hoping that salvation will arrive in time.

That is the picture that comes to mind when we hear the word *famine*. But that is only one kind of famine, one kind of hunger. Spiritually, we can experience a famine as well. As the Bible tells us: *"Behold, days are coming, says God, when I will send a famine in the land, not a famine for bread, nor a thirst for water, but to hear the words of God."* [2]

---

[1] Ruth 1:1

[2] Amos 8:11

When we lack Divine inspiration and blessings in our lives, we experience spiritual hunger. We sense that our souls have been depleted. We starve for spiritual sustenance, and this torment can translate into an emotional turmoil that has physical repercussions. At such times, the worst of human behavior can result.

Such was the situation in the time of Judges, a colorful period in Biblical history, dating from approximately 1200 BCE to 880 BCE. This was the time of Deborah and Barak, of Samson and Delilah, of Chana and Samuel. The Israelites had settled the land of Israel, but had not yet established a monarchy. Instead, the Bible tells us, *"Everyone did what was right in his own eyes."* [3]

If our eyes don't deceive us, doing what is right in our eyes is a wonderful thing. It means that everyone is doing the right thing – living by God's law – and that consequently, God is keeping His part of the bargain – delivering rain at the proper time to ensure healthy and abundant crops that fill the storehouses with grain, wine and oil.[4]

But clearly that is not what is going on when the Book of Ruth begins. There is a famine, indicating that God has withdrawn His blessings. Everyone is doing what is *"right in his own eyes,"* living according to his own rules, not according to the law of God.

Here we see clearly the relationship between nature and nurture: acts of nature reflect the lack of caring, both from below to above – with people not caring about God and His law, and from above to below – with God responding in kind. When God

---

[3] Judges 21:25

[4] Deuteronomy 11:14

suspends His blessings and the spiritual light of His presence dims, the famine, which is evident in nature, is also evident in spirit. Thus the situation spirals out of control; first people violate God's law, hating their neighbor, coveting what is not theirs, cheating in business. Next, in the presence of such arrogance and in the absence of remorse, God withdraws. Ultimately, the withdrawal of His light leads to even greater spiritual darkness.

Such a cycle can be seen in a famous Talmudic tale about *Choni Ha-Me'agel*, Choni the Circle Drawer, who lived in the first century BCE. A severe drought, linked in some way to the behavior of the people, afflicted the land. As the drought lingered and worsened, the people despaired and became increasingly introspective, wondering how they could alleviate their desperate situation. They finally turned to Choni, a righteous man, and asked him to pray for rain. He meditated for three days and drew a circle around himself. He declared: "I will not move from here until Thou hast mercy upon Thy children."[5] Through Choni's meditative intervention, a certain equilibrium and balance came over the city and those who dwelled in it. Rain began to fall. Choni took a stand – as we shall see, Ruth also takes a stand.

This relationship between human behavior and the state of the natural world is alluded to at the very beginning of the Book of Ruth. Biblical commentators tell us that the famine described in the first sentence of the Book of Ruth was not only physical but also spiritual, moral and ethical. Judges were easily bribed. Their decisions, influenced by greed, were distortions of the truth and

---

[5] *Ta'anit* 23a

bereft of mercy. The *Midrash*, reading the Hebrew text literally as, *"In the days of the judgment of the Judges,"* [6] tells us that the Judges may have judged, but they were also judged – unfavorably – by the people. The Talmud laments: "Woe unto the generation whose Judges are judged, and woe to the generation whose Judges deserve to be judged."[7]

Today the equivalent of the Judges who deserve to be judged are the powerful figures who control our lives – such as the CEOs whose decisions to downsize or to engineer mergers negatively affect millions of employees. How do those in positions of power deal with the people whose lives they control?

I am acquainted with a young couple in a difficult financial situation who are living from paycheck to paycheck. Recently, the wife suffered the loss of her beloved grandmother and she asked for time off to attend the funeral. But her manager, unbelievable as it may sound, told her that if she took off that day, she need not bother coming back – she would lose her job. People who so lack compassion lose the respect of their employees; the morale of their workers plummets.

When a company's health wobbles, the first to jump ship are sometimes those in positions of power who are privy to inside

---

[6] Ruth 1:1

[7] *Bava Batra* 15b

information – they seek to save themselves, not caring what happens to others. This, too, can be seen in the story of Ruth.

Chapter 2

TUNNEL VISION

"And a man of Bethlehem in Judah went to dwell in the fields of Moab, he and his wife and two sons. The man's name was Elimelech, his wife's name was Naomi, the names of his two sons were Machlon and Kilyon...." [1]

The *"man of Bethlehem"* – in Hebrew *ish mi-Beit Lechem* – is Biblical code for "a wealthy man" from Bethlehem, which at that time was one of the finest places to live in Israel. Rashi,[2] a famed eleventh-century Biblical commentator, suggests that Elimelech fled in time of famine because he did not want to be besieged by hordes of hungry people coming to him for help. As a result, he was quick to abandon his home and his country – Israel, the Promised Land. That he was a miser is further suggested by his destination: Moab.

Moab was a nation of miserly people. We know from the Book of Deuteronomy[3] that instead of greeting travelers on the way to

---

[1] Ruth 1:1–2

[2] Rashi, Ruth 1:1

[3] Deuteronomy 2:28, 23:5

the Promised Land with water and bread, as was the custom of the day, the Moabites sold them these basic necessities.

What sort of person would sell a cup of water to a thirsty traveler? What sort of person would take advantage of the physical or mental exhaustion of another to make a profit? The same sort of person who today raises prices of necessities following a natural disaster. The same sort of person who today demands exorbitant prices for life-saving medication or treatment. Health care benefits can be like water; they can mean life or death. "Selling bread and water" is more prevalent today than we think.

These were the kind of people among whom a miserly man like Elimelech could feel right at home; no one would question his behavior in abandoning his neighbors in time of need. So Elimelech went from a place where people were bothering him to a place where people didn't want to be bothered.

His name and the names of his sons provide further clues as to their character traits. Elimelech can mean "unto me, I am a king" or "to myself, I am king." Elimelech had two sons, Machlon, meaning "Ill," and Kilyon, meaning "Destruction." It is not clear whether these are their actual names or if this is what the Bible chooses to call them. What is clear is that the Bible intends to convey the message that Elimelech, this arrogant man who had no empathy for others while they starved, has fathered and engendered illness and destruction.

In contrast, his wife's name is Naomi, meaning "pleasant." However, her benign feminine energy is not strong enough to overcome the dark energy of the three men in her family. The men dominate and Naomi cannot prevail.

From a psychological standpoint, we see here a family system that is out of balance. And indeed, it is well known that family life is significantly affected in conscious and unconscious ways whenever there is an imbalance of either masculine or feminine energy. The challenge is to try, no matter what the number of men or women in a family, to achieve a balance.

In this case, negative male energy predominates. The Bible subtly hints that it is Elimelech who is making all the decisions for his family. We are told that *"the **man**, Elimelech, went to dwell in the fields of Moab, he, and his wife, and his two sons."* [4] We are not told that *"they* went" together.

Elimelech exemplifies the kind of head of family who dominates and controls others, who decides what is best for all without asking each of them. Oftentimes what he perceives to be best for all is really what is best for him.

I know of a family that underwent a traumatic move from Texas to Norway when the father was offered a promotion and a hefty raise in salary by his employer, a major oil company based in Texas but drilling in the North Sea. When his wife and children objected to the move, pointing out that they would be torn from friends and extended family and forced to learn a new language and culture, he claimed that he was doing it "all for the family." The hefty raise would buy them things they could not afford now, the move would make the children more worldly and multi-cultural, and the benefits would far outweigh the temporary discomfort. "All for the family" was really a mask for his own

---

[4] Ruth 1:1

selfishness and ego gratification. He got his way. But two years later, his marriage was on the verge of collapsing and his oldest child was seriously abusing alcohol, while his younger child was becoming more and more estranged from him.

Another example that comes to mind is that of a woman whose mother suffered a mild stroke, which impaired her mobility somewhat. Unable to drive and get around without help, the mother found herself quite isolated, especially since she lived in the suburbs and the daughter and extended family lived in the city. Many solutions might have been found to remedy this situation. The daughter might have invited the mother to move into her own spacious home or to find an assisted-living apartment nearby. However, she did not want her mother so close. So instead, she bought her mother a television set for every room. The daughter explained that this decreased her mother's loneliness as she now heard voices everywhere she turned. It was a quick, cheap solution, but it hardly met the mother's needs for human companionship. What mattered to the daughter, however, was that her own guilt was diminished.

Such people often suffer from narrow vision – what we today call "tunnel vision" – their egos blinding them to the true perception of reality. Indeed, these are just the kind of people who err when "doing what is right in their own eyes."

Most people who have narrow vision in sizing up reality often judge others negatively. They observe only the externals – the physical appearance, ethnicity and socio-economic status of another. Their vision is both narrow and superficial. These are the people who cannot give others the benefit of the doubt, who judge and disparage and cannot see the other's point of view.

Narrow vision can be a dangerous, progressive malady. People with narrow vision can box themselves in like Elimelech, who ultimately became the loser in the end, because having narrow vision nearly always leads to destruction. Specifically, Elimelech did not want people knocking on his door. He just didn't want to be disturbed.

Sometimes in the normal course of life, family responsibilities, professional duties and personal concerns may overwhelm an individual. Undoubtedly, one has to establish boundaries in order to survive. However, oftentimes the greatest reward comes when people put forth tremendous effort, especially when they think they have nothing more to give.

I am reminded of an overworked physician who was finally able to find the time to go on a European vacation with his family. He made his plane reservation in the name of "Mr." Smith, not "Dr." Smith, because he didn't want to be bothered by anyone seeking medical advice or care. But mid-flight from Los Angeles to London, a fellow passenger began to complain of chest pains and shortness of breath. One of the flight attendants asked, "Is there a doctor on board?" No one responded. No one moved. Dr. Smith sat in silence, hoping against hope that another physician was on the plane. As moments passed and the passenger continued to complain of symptoms, Dr. Smith felt torn. He did not want to become involved. But he could not sit by idly while someone might be in danger or even dying.

He identified himself as a physician and rushed to the man's side. He comforted him, reassured him and gave him some nitroglycerin tablets that he had in his carry-on bag. He was relieved to discover that the passenger could make it safely all the way to London.

The next day, as Dr. Smith sat in his hotel room in London, he felt calm and peaceful. He reflected on what had happened the day before. He realized that up until the episode on the airplane, he had experienced limited vision, tunnel vision. His main concern had been the narrow practice of medicine in his office setting. Now he'd been forced to think about why he had gone into medicine in the first place. This expanded vision enabled him to appreciate the privilege, as well as the responsibility, of his life's calling.

That is what Elimelech failed to recognize. In his move from Bethlehem to Moab, he cared only about not being bothered by people less fortunate than himself. He wanted to be left alone, without people knocking on his door. And he got his wish, but not in the way he anticipated. He ultimately lost everything dear to him, including his life.

Chapter 3

LOSS

"Elimelech, Naomi's husband, died, and she was left with her two sons. They married Moabite women, one of whom was named Orpah, and the name of the second was Ruth; and they lived there [in Moab] about ten years." [1]

Elimelech fled his homeland in order to prevent loss, yet he suffered the ultimate loss – he lost his life. After his death, his sons made no plans to return to Israel. Instead, they married Moabite women, not women from among the tribes of Israel.

They chose as their brides two princesses, the daughters of Eglon, the king of Moab.[2] The fact that they managed to marry royalty seems to indicate that the stature and materialism of the father had been passed down to the sons. The king would not have given his daughters in marriage to just anyone, so it appears that Machlon and Kilyon were very wealthy and prominent members of society. Their marriage into the king's court further elevated their status.

---

[1] Ruth 1:3–4

[2] *Ruth Rabbah* 2:9

These two noble women thus became Naomi's daughters-in-law. These two brides of the Book of Ruth have vastly different names, each of which foreshadows their biblical stories and the images we have of them. Orpah, who marries Kilyon, has a name meaning "nape of the neck," and the *Midrash*[3] suggests she was so named because later, at the hour of decision-making, she turned her back on her mother-in-law. In English, Ruth means "compassionate." We still utilize the word "ruthless" to indicate someone who is lacking this trait. Ruth responded to her mother-in-law's plight with compassion.

Ruth can also mean "satiated with song" or "filled with praise." The spiritual energy of Ruth eventually came to inspire her future descendant, King David – known as "the sweet singer of Israel" – to compose some of the most beautiful and enduring hymns to God: the Psalms.

The marriages of Machlon and Kilyon demonstrate that these sons responded to the loss of their father not with despondency, but with a desire to renew life. I know of a man who lost his wife to cancer and after three years still had not been able to let go of his grief. So sad was he that when his only son married, he could not be happy even then. In the photo album of the wedding he stands out – a morose face, an island of sadness in a sea of brilliant smiles. His story has a happy ending, however. When his son fathered a child, the presence of a new life finally brought him out of his depression. Energized by the life force of his baby grandson, he was able to open himself to new experience. He

---

[3] *Ruth Rabbah* 2:4

began to socialize more, met a wonderful woman and eventually remarried.

Bringing new life into the world was not the destiny of either Machlon or Kilyon. After ten years, neither had fathered a child. And then they both died: *"The two of them, Machlon and Kilyon also died, and the woman was bereft of her two children and of her husband."* [4]

Naomi has suffered the ultimate loss – her entire family is gone. Her husband is dead, her only two sons are dead, and there are no grandchildren to carry on any of their names.

The depth of Naomi's sorrow can be gleaned from her very own words. On her arrival in Bethlehem, she says, *"Do not call me Naomi [pleasant]; call me Mara [bitter]."* [5] But her response to her unquestionably bitter fate is uplifting – she *chooses to be kind*, as we shall see. Generally, bitter people in today's world tend to spread their bitterness around, while happy people are mostly kind. Despite her difficult circumstances, however, Naomi spreads kindness.

But how can we transform bitterness into kindness as Naomi did?

Dr. Viktor Frankl (1905–1997), the founder of logotherapy, believed that when you attribute personal meaning to your suffering, that meaning sets your experience in a different perspective, makes it endurable, and eventually helps guide your

---

[4] Ruth 1:5

[5] Ruth 1:20

life. Frankl, in his classic work, *Man's Search for Meaning*,[6] described his own wartime experiences, which helped shape his philosophy. In his darkest hours, what helped to keep him going was his desire to find his wife and family again and to transform his terrible experiences in some positive way in order to benefit humankind.

Carl Gustav Jung (1875–1961), founder of one of the great schools of psychotherapy, came to a similar conclusion about how to cope with life's challenges. In his words, "The experience of the Self is always a defeat for the ego."[7] In other words, when we have a *transpersonal* perspective, when we no longer feel alone in our psyche and in the universe, the ups and downs of life take on new and broader meanings.

Such a perspective is the only thing that allows Naomi to go forward in the face of the multiple tragedies she has suffered. Instead of wallowing in self-pity, Naomi specifically *uses* her despair and her bereavement to give herself a new start in life. Only a transpersonal approach to pain and suffering allows for such a life journey with new beginnings.

Loss and suffering are part of life. No one escapes such experiences. What matters is how we deal with them. One of the most inspirational examples of a positive response to suffering is that of the Klausenburger Rebbe, Rabbi Jekuthiel Judah

---

[6] Frankl, V. *Man's Search for Meaning: An Introduction to Logotherapy.* NY: Pocket Books, 1939.

[7] Jung, C.G. *Mysterium Coniunctionis.* 2nd ed. [Bollingen Series XX]. Princeton, NJ: Princeton University Press, 1963, p. 546.

Halberstam.[8] Having lost his wife and eleven children in the Holocaust, having seen his entire family wiped out, he remarried and had more children – perhaps the greatest statement of his faith in the hope that goodness would prevail in the world. Furthermore, he chose to dedicate his life to acts of loving-kindness. Among these, he established Laniado Hospital in Israel, a very special institution where no patient is ever turned away and every employee is treated with dignity and respect. At the dedication ceremony for Laniado, which I was privileged to attend, the Rebbe said: "Certain commandments and obligations take on more importance after a catastrophe, after losses. You may ask why a Hassidic Rebbe is building a hospital? After World War II and the *Shoah*, the most important obligation is to be kind and to instill hope in others."

Just as the Klausenburger Rebbe had hope, so does the institution he founded. Never was this demonstrated so dramatically as after the Passover massacre of 2002. On the first night of that holiday, as a crowd of 300 people gathered at the Park Hotel in Netanya to celebrate the Passover Seder, a terrible suicide and homicide explosion ripped through the building. The blast was so loud that it was heard throughout the city.

Within minutes, the first victims had arrived at Laniado Hospital, located about three minutes away from the hotel. Seventy-three wounded were brought in for treatment, twenty-two of them severely wounded. It was very difficult for the staff to deal with such horrible injuries, many of them to women and

---

[8] Lifschitz, J. *The Klausenburger Rebbe: The War Years*. NY: Feldheim, 2003.

children. Asked how the dedicated Laniado team coped with the many wounded they had to treat, Dr. Yoel First, head of Laniado's Disaster Response Unit, said: "We are believers. We never give up hope that each new attack will be the last."[9]

Likewise, in the Book of Ruth, Naomi does not give up hope. She is a model of remarkable strength. She is able to arise, despite her agony and sorrow. She is bereft, yet finds strength in her bereavement. She uses this strength to do what her husband and sons failed to do. Her life no longer dominated by their choices, she resolves to return to the Land of Israel: *"She [Naomi] then arose along with her daughters-in-law to return from the fields of Moab...."* [10]

Naomi's daughters-in-law accompany her out of town, but then she directs them to turn back; she has nothing more to offer them. Orpah kisses Naomi – she will make a life for herself in Moab and ultimately become known as the ancestor of the giant Goliath.[11] But Ruth clings to Naomi, refusing to let go. In that moment, the nobility of Ruth's character emerges, and it is far greater and more significant than her princess nobility of birth. Indeed, she and her sister have the very same lineage, but Ruth's

---

[9] Quoted in "Snatching Lives from the Angel of Death," by Linda Feinberg. Posted on the Aish HaTorah website, www.aish.com, 2002.

[10] Ruth 1:6

[11] *Sotah* 42b

character is quite different. From this point, we begin to focus on what enables Ruth to accompany her mother-in-law, Naomi, and to convert to Judaism.

Chapter 4

CONVERSION

As Naomi encourages Ruth to follow the lead of Orpah, her sister-in-law, and remain in her land with her own people, Ruth responds: *"Do not urge me to desert you, to turn away from you. For wherever you go, I shall go; wherever you lodge, I will lodge; your people are my people, and your God is my God."* [1]

At the essence of the Book of Ruth is the story of Ruth's conversion, perhaps one of the most famous such episodes in history. Biblical commentators differ as to when Ruth actually converted. The most commonly accepted approach is that of Rashi, who believes that Ruth converted at the moment she made the above declarations to Naomi as they were on the road from Moab to Bethlehem.[2] Rashi further comments: "Come and see how dear the proselytes are before the Holy One, Blessed be He. As soon as Ruth decided to convert, the Bible compared her to

---

[1] Ruth 1:16

[2] Rashi states (on Ruth 1:12) that Ruth and Orpah "were gentiles and had not yet converted" during the time they were married to Naomi's sons.

Naomi by stating, 'and the *two* of them went on until they came to Bethlehem.' "[3]

How did Ruth find the desire and strength to embark on this spiritual and physical journey with Naomi? Perhaps we can infer the answer from what is not stated explicitly, but what presumably took place during the time that Naomi lived in Moab with her daughters-in-law.

Both Ruth and Orpah were clearly attached to Naomi. Even though Orpah did not return with her, she initially wanted to. This suggests that both Ruth and Orpah were especially well-treated by their mother-in-law. Naomi must have regarded both of her daughters-in-law as individuals, rather than as stereotypical Moabite women. She did not pigeonhole them and make assumptions about them based on their families of origin.

Every family has a complex history. No one is "pure-blooded." Any attempts to deny or to control access to such information are usually based on fear. I have met numerous families who try their best to check up on a potential son or daughter-in-law in every possible way, including medically, taking into account specific issues such as fertility. Some parents feel that by checking on someone's health background, they can feel more secure about a couple's potential to procreate and make them grandparents.

In truth, however, such knowledge does not provide any kind of power. I think of one mother who tried very hard to dissuade her daughter from marrying a man with diabetes. "His disease is so unpredictable," she told her daughter. "You know how many

---

[3] Rashi, Ruth 1:19

complications there can be, including some very serious ones." Nevertheless, the daughter insisted on proceeding with her marriage. Her husband has proven to be a wonderful, supportive husband. He does more than anyone could have imagined, for in a great twist of fate, his wife has developed multiple sclerosis, so that now *he* is the one who must care for *her*.

It is important to withhold our judgment of others, even in our heart of hearts. When we interact in this way, we will surely bring out the best in the other person. But this is not always easy to do. When we approach someone else with an open heart, we are relinquishing control – of the past and of our feelings – and that is a very great challenge. However, control is only an illusion, as the above story illustrates. We merely strive for control in an effort to reduce our own anxieties.

When it comes to religious conversion, some people cannot – or will not – welcome the newcomer to the faith with an open heart, recognizing the person as a legitimate member of the community. Just recently, I spoke to a Jewish mother who was distraught because her son had married a woman who converted from Catholicism to Judaism. "I just can't accept her," she told me. Even after I reminded her of the story of Ruth, this mother was not swayed. "It doesn't matter," she said. "I can't help looking at her as a gentile."

How different this woman's behavior is from that of Naomi, who was able to relate to Ruth as an individual, not as a stereotype. Furthermore, Naomi was undoubtedly impressed with the special qualities that she perceived in Ruth. Naomi must have quickly noted her daughter-in-law's kindness, virtue, modesty and potential for spiritual growth. Naomi accepted Ruth wholeheartedly and lovingly. Why else would Ruth have been so willing and eager to follow her? Why else would Ruth choose to cleave to her, especially after Naomi tries so hard to dissuade Ruth and Orpah from following her? *"Go return, each of you to her mother's home.... Turn back, my daughters, why should you come with me?... Turn back, my daughters, go your way...."* [4]

Despite Naomi's repeated pleas, Ruth perseveres in her desire to remain with her mother-in-law. Ruth then makes her famous declarations of loyalty and faith, regarded as her statement of conversion: *"For wherever you go, I shall go; wherever you lodge, I will lodge; your people are my people, and your God is my God."* [5]

One might suppose that conversion involves only a personal relationship to God. However, Ruth's declarations refer, according to rabbinical interpretation, to other matters as well, including acceptance of many specific Jewish laws. This is because the process of conversion is quite comprehensive. Initially, a potential convert is excited about the prospect of intense personal transformation. However, conversion also entails the acceptance of new religious laws and responsibilities. Some of them are quite substantive and require changes in lifestyle. In our times, it would not suffice to point out the joys of eating bagels and lox on Sunday morning or joining a Jewish country club or sharing a joyful Passover Seder with loved ones. Judaism involves many challenging responsibilities. For example, someone who converts

---

[4] Ruth 1:8, 1:11, 1:12

[5] Ruth 1:16

to Judaism must realize that he or she can no longer frequent a favorite restaurant and partake of non-kosher food and wine that is served there. It is therefore important to inform a potential convert of both easy and difficult laws. Making sure that he or she understands and accepts such laws is vital to prevent possible backsliding.

When a person converts, he or she might still feel an emotional attachment with the past so as to think, "I want to convert and connect with the Jewish people and still maintain a connection with my people and my former way of life." Such feelings are quite prevalent in modern American society. Some people feel that they can have both Chanukah candles and a Christmas tree in their living room. After all, the tree evokes good, warm memories. But one cannot honor two gods.

Ruth understands this. She resolves wholeheartedly to leave her former ways and her former people behind. That, of course, means her royal Moabite family. But it is worthwhile to consider who Ruth's people *really* are.

We know that her origins go back to Lot. Lot, in turn, was Abraham's nephew, the son of Abraham's brother, Haran. Ruth is now undertaking a journey similar to the one taken by her illustrious ancestor, Abraham, the first Jew and the first convert. Like him, she is fulfilling God's commandment: *"Go forth [lech lecha] from your country, and from your birthplace, and from your father's house, to the land that I will show you."* [6]

---

[6] Genesis 12:1

When Ruth says to Naomi, *"wherever you go, I shall go,"* she is stating that she will undertake a going forth – a *lech lecha* – just as Abraham did. She is saying, "I will go forth, whatever that entails." And the rewards of such a journey can be great. Abraham, after undertaking his journey, became the first Jew. When Ruth became a Jew, she ultimately paved the way for the coming of the Messiah.

It is difficult to appreciate the tremendous internal strength and fortitude that Ruth displays in her declarations of conversion. She demonstrates unbelievable determination in drastically changing her patterns of behavior. In this process, she finds strength and direction in her close and wonderful relationship with Naomi, her mother-in-law, mentor and soul friend. Ruth observes Naomi's compassionate character and her ability to transcend the most terrible losses and suffering. She learns from Naomi's personal and interpersonal behavior, as well as from Naomi's words. At the same time, Naomi intuits Ruth's spirituality, her great character and potential to successfully overcome any obstacles, internal and external, in her path to conversion and a new life.

Ruth's promise to cling to Naomi and remain at her side[7] is particularly significant. She is telling Naomi, "I will not abandon you. I will be with you." Her language echoes God's words to those who experience challenging times.[8]

And Naomi is certainly challenged at this point. She is confronting tremendous difficulties and losses, having suffered the death of her husband and sons. Naomi has even spoken movingly

---

[7] Ruth 1:17

[8] Genesis 28:15; Exodus 3:14

to Ruth about how she feels in the face of these tragedies: *"...against me is directed the hand of God."* [9]

Naomi is accurately depicting her inner bitterness. It is impossible for her *not* to feel the way she does in the wake of losing her husband and sons. However, Naomi's greatness may be seen in her outward actions, no matter what her state of mind or circumstances. She manages to emerge from her depression and improve the quality of her life, as well as the lives of those around her.

Naomi's exceptional response to tragedy is apparent to Ruth. Therefore, Ruth refuses to let go of Naomi and to abandon her, no matter what difficulties lie ahead of them. The story of Ruth thus conveys a lesson about family life and real family relationships. It is relatively easy to help a stranger. It doesn't take that much time or commitment. For example, a physician may hold a patient's hand for just a few minutes and then prescribe some medication. The greater challenge is how to be compassionate within one's own family and to *remain* at someone's side for as long as necessary.

Ruth rises to the challenge of being there for Naomi during Naomi's most difficult hours. Specifically, because God's hand is directed *against* Naomi, Ruth's hand *reaches out* to Naomi. By helping Naomi, she is also extending her hand out to God.

---

[9] Ruth 1:13

Chapter 5

WHERE IS GOD?

"My distress is great on your account, for against me is directed the hand of God." [1]

As I write these words on Sunday, February 2, 2003, the entire world is reeling from the tragic events of yesterday – the loss of the space shuttle Columbia and all of its seven astronauts. These were good people, men and women of different colors and faiths, husbands and wives, mothers and fathers, scientists engaged in a mission for the betterment of humankind. Yet in one moment, their lives came to an abrupt, fiery end. Many in the world community looked on in horror, asking, "Where is God?"

That same question is often on the lips of people facing personal losses – illness, pain and death. Such suffering is universal and people have experienced it since the beginning of time. However, their responses to suffering can and do vary.

Early in our story, for example, Naomi tells her daughters-in-law: *"My distress is great on your account, for against me is directed the hand of God."* [2] She also tells the women of Bethlehem: *"...call me*

---

[1] Ruth 1:13

[2] Ruth 1:13

Mara [embittered one], for most bitterly has God dealt with me. I had gone forth full but God has brought me back empty; why call me Naomi, when God has testified against me and the Almighty [has brought] catastrophe upon me?" [3]

In our story, it is clear that God is central to all of nature and that His blessings are seen as essential to daily life. Yet, it is likewise apparent that the people in this story also view the painful aspects of life as stemming from the will of God.

In her heartfelt cries of anguish, Naomi is expressing sentiments that the Prophets also articulated. The concept of an all-powerful God leads inevitably to statements such as those recorded by Isaiah, for example, who quotes God as saying: *"I form the light, and create darkness: I make peace, and create evil; I, the Lord, do all these things."* [4] Jeremiah similarly asks rhetorically in the Book of Lamentations: *"Out of the mouth of the Most High do not both good and evil come?"* [5]

However, the Book of Ruth *is* different from most of the other books of the Bible where people routinely dialogue with God. (For example, in the Torah – the Five Books of Moses – the phrase, *"And God spoke to Moses, saying…"* appears 175 times.) But in the Book of Ruth, there are *no* recorded instances of God speaking directly to the people or their dialoguing with God. However, God is not at all absent. On the contrary, this text is filled with the presence of God, Who permeates the lives of

---

[3] Ruth 1:20–21

[4] Isaiah 45:7

[5] Lamentations 3:38

everyone in this story. His existence is never questioned; it is understood, lived and breathed. This absolute belief in one transcendent, everlasting God is a core foundation of faith, as codified by Maimonides in his Thirteen Principles.[6] This is a view of the world that is to be accepted by any potential convert.

Ruth clearly understands the world in this way. And in her story, it is not only the principal characters view God as an integral part of their lives. All of the people, no matter what their roles or status – villagers, women, harvesters – speak of an immanent God, One who is intimately concerned with their daily lives and well-being. Their language not only reflects their understanding of the world; it also helps to *build* a world that is God-directed and inspired. As Carl Gustav Jung reminded himself daily with the inscription above his door, "Bidden or not bidden, God is present."

At the very beginning of the story of Ruth, we see that everything in nature – such as famine and recovery from it – is understood as part of the Divine will: *"She [Naomi] then arose with her daughters-in-law, in order to return from the fields of Moab, for she had heard in the fields of Moab that God had cared for his people to give them food."*[7]

Furthermore, people routinely bless each other in the Name of God, and blessings abound in this story. When Naomi tries to

---

[6] Maimonides. "Thirteen Principles of Faith," in the *Daily Prayer Book*, translated and annotated with an introduction by Philip Birnbaum, NY, Hebrew Publishing Company, 1999, pp. 153–156.

[7] Ruth 1:6

prevail upon Ruth and Orpah to return to the homes of their mothers, she adds: *"Go, return, each of you to her mother's home; may God deal kindly with you as you have dealt with the dead and with me. May God grant you that you may find comfort each in the home of her new husband...."* [8]

Blessings such as Naomi's can be powerful indeed, and we, too, have the ability to bestow them. Our words will continue to resonate in the ears and the heart of the listener long after they are uttered. One young woman I know, a highly successful scientist, told me that a childhood blessing from her father continues to guide her in all she does. "I was in the sixth or seventh grade," she said, "and I lacked self-confidence. I felt that I could never be as bright or successful as either of my parents. And my father, a world-renowned surgeon, must have sensed what I was feeling. He wrote a note to me on my birthday. It said: 'To Miriam, the light of my life. You are so special and dear to us. You have wonderful talents and qualities. I know that you will follow your heart and become the Miriam that *you* are meant to be.' I still have the card, even though I don't need to read it. My father's words are engraved on my heart."

The most remarkable thing about Naomi's blessings is that she is able to give them at all after what she has experienced. She has lost her husband. She has buried two sons. She has returned to her native land, not sure of her future or even where her next meal will come from. She does not know how she will be received or by whom. Although she finds comfort from her devoted daughter-in-

---

[8] Ruth 1:8–9

law, she remains lonely. But through all these trials and tribulations, Naomi's faith and her belief remain; she never loses faith in God. And Ruth, although she, too, experienced the supreme challenges of life, nevertheless stays with Naomi, converts and says, *"For wherever you go, I shall go, where you lodge, I will lodge, your people are my people, and your God is my God."* [9]

That is because for Naomi and Ruth, like so many others in the Bible, God is a *living presence*, with Whom one can engage in dialogue, during both the good and the challenging times. She has attained what James Fowler categorizes as the highest level of faith development.[10]

Therein lies the secret of how Naomi, Ruth and others in this story deal with all that confronts them on a personal and communal level. Theirs is a living God, Who is with them in the good times and the bad. By living their lives in an intimate, ongoing relationship and dialogue with Him, they find strength and sustenance to continue along their journey. That is the secret to their survival and it can be ours as well. The Book of Ruth, therefore, does not need to record dialogues with God, for they are implied and understood. People in such a deep, committed relationship with the Divine do not limit themselves to dialogue from time to time – their entire lives are a dialogue with God.

As Naomi shows kindness to Ruth and others, she is continuing God's work. For the very first words uttered by God in

---

[9] Ruth 1:16

[10] Fowler, James W. *Stages of Faith: The Psychology of Human Development and the Quest for Meaning.* NY: Harper & Row, 1981.

the Bible are: *"Let there be light."* [11] Through her actions, Naomi is bringing more light to the world. Each of us has that same opportunity, and it behooves us to be aware of the need for such behavior, in particular, as we relate to those who are weak and powerless, those who do not have a protector.

This living relationship is beautifully articulated by the late Rabbi Dr. Adolf (Avraham) Altmann, former Chief Rabbi of Trier, Germany, in his seminal article, "The Meaning and Soul of 'Hear, O Israel'."[12] In it, he explores the *Shema*, the "Hear, O Israel" prayer, which is the core statement of Judaic faith. Rabbi Altmann refers to the uninterrupted voice of God, which spoke from Sinai but can still be heard today:

> God's Sinai voice has never turned silent for us; its echo continues throughout time…. If the voice from Sinai ever ceases for us, so will the life-pervading content of its message, and our ethical being will fade away…. Out of the call of another human being, God's voice can also speak to us.

Rabbi Altmann goes on to state:

---

[11] Genesis 1:3

[12] Altmann, A. (1928). "Sin und Seele des 'Hore Israel'." ("The Meaning and Soul of 'Hear, O Israel'.") Berlin: *Jeschurun* (ed. By Joseph Wohlgemuth), 11/12. Translated from the German by Barbara R. Algin and edited by Rabbi Levi Meier. In Meier, L. *Jewish Values in Jungian Psychology.* Lanham, MD: University Press of America, 1991, pp. 61–62.

There are voices and calls which sound out loud, yet one fails to hear them, and there are others that make no sound at all, yet they are heard. The human without ethics passes by what cries out most in life without hearing, whereas one of high moral character hears even the most subdued call and traces its source. He knows that what is most quiet sometimes speaks loudest…. If no one else hears the silent cry of the humiliated, the powerless hidden victims, the Jew must hear it; that is the noblest ethical significance of the "Hear, O Israel." Through the silent walls of hard prison cells hear the sighs, Israel; out of the lonely huts of deserted widows and orphans, from the bed of pain of the sick and suffering, from the silently borne anguish of those rejected or denied justice… you as a Jew must hear the cries of pain, without their having to be emitted. The cry of suffering is the cry of God, calling out from its victims to you….[13]

Rabbi Altmann gets to the heart of what is expected of us as ethical human beings. The voice of God continues to speak to us if we would but attune our ears and listen to it. And that listening must lead to *action*. In the story of Ruth, we read of how the House of David, the forerunner of the Messiah, came to be. It was established through the righteous *actions* of those who heard the word of God and followed it every moment and every day of their lives.

---

[13] Ibid., p. 63.

Where is God? He is everywhere. Even in the worst of times, each of us, like Naomi and her family, can be guided by His living presence and moral lessons. Naomi, Ruth and the others in this story who conduct themselves in this way are great role models for each and every one of us.

If we read the Book of Ruth on a simple level, we may think of it as a narrative, and quite a beautiful one at that. But it is also a text of ethical guidance. It presents the story of a great miracle, one just as awesome as any of the others recorded in the Bible. For after all of the tragedies and all of the losses that Ruth and Naomi experience, the Name of God flows freely from their lips. It is their relationship with a living God that enables them to continue to relate to everyone with an abundance of kindness. No wonder they are given a second chance to repair the mistakes of the past. No wonder they are privileged to usher in the redemption of humankind.

Part II: KINDNESS

The Book of Ruth (Summary of Chapter 2)

Having arrived in Bethlehem with her mother-in-law, Naomi, Ruth goes out to glean what remains in the field after the harvesters have passed, as is the custom of the poor. She happens upon the field of Boaz, who is a nephew of Elimelech, her late father-in-law, though she does not know that. When Boaz sees her in his field, he asks about her and learns who she is. He is most kind to her, urging her to glean only in his field, and he instructs his workers to leave extra grain for her to glean. Boaz also invites her to share his food and water. When Ruth returns home with a supply of grain, she tells Naomi about her experiences. Naomi informs Ruth that Boaz is a relative and a potential marriage partner for her. Following Naomi's advice, Ruth continues to glean in Boaz's field until the end of the harvest.

Chapter 6

HEAVENLY AND EARTHLY MARRIAGE

As we have seen, Ruth's conversion takes places as she cleaves to her mother-in-law, Naomi, accompanying her back to Bethlehem. Ruth declares: *"For wherever you go, I shall go; wherever you lodge, I will lodge; your people are my people, and your God is my God."* [1]

Ruth demonstrates extraordinary loyalty and devotion to her mother-in-law, Naomi. In some of the most beautiful language in the Bible, Ruth expresses her determination to stay by Naomi's side, convert and become part of Naomi's people. That decision of Ruth's has profound and lasting consequences.

Converting to Judaism is a holy experience. It is a process of great personal transformation and significance, similar in some respects to entering into a marriage relationship. As a matter of fact, the language of the Book of Ruth reminds the reader of the commonalities between conversion and marriage.

For example, marriage is described, early in Genesis, as follows: *"Therefore shall a man leave his father and his mother and shall cleave to his wife and they shall be one flesh."* [2] That very same verb – cleaving

---

[1] Ruth 1:16

[2] Genesis 2:24

כִּי אֶל אֲשֶׁר תֵּלְכִי אֵלֵךְ, וּבַאֲשֶׁר
אֵלִין, עַמֵּךְ עַמִּי, וֵאלֹהַיִךְ אֱלֹהָי

עַל כֵּן יַעֲזָב אִישׁ אֶת אָבִיו וְאֶת אִמּוֹ
וְדָבַק בְּאִשְׁתּוֹ וְהָיוּ לְבָשָׂר אֶחָד

– is used to describe Ruth's actions when she chooses to return with her mother-in-law, Naomi, to a new land and a new faith: "Ruth **cleaved** to her."[3] And that same verb is used again in Deuteronomy to describe the loving relationship between the Jewish people and God: "You that did *cleave* unto the Lord your God are alive every one of you this day."[4]

The relationship between marriage and conversion can also be clearly seen in the symbolic ritual of the *mikvah*, the ritual bath. On a monthly basis during marriage, a Jewish woman immerses herself in a *mikvah* after her menstrual period, so that she may be sexually intimate with her husband. Similarly, before conversion, the potential convert immerses in the *mikvah*. The symbolism is clear: When one converts, one is, as it were, giving birth to oneself spiritually and participating in a symbolic wedding ceremony with God.

During both the conversion ceremony and the marriage ceremony, similar promises are made. For example, Ruth's famous declarations of love and loyalty to Naomi[5] are understood to mean: "No matter what happens, no matter what ups and downs life brings, despite life's tribulations – even if unanticipated life challenges continue – I will still remain a Jew." That same degree of *commitment* – that same willingness to weather all seasons together with the other – is also essential to marriage.

---

[3] Ruth 1:14 וַתִּדְבַּק בָּהּ

[4] Deuteronomy 4:4

[5] Ruth 1:16–17

After Ruth convinces Naomi of her sincerity and determination to follow her no matter what may happen, Ruth becomes a convert to Judaism. The text then describes how Ruth and Naomi journey along together: *"So the two of them went on...."*[6] This Hebrew expression is reminiscent of the closeness of a bride and groom as they begin their walk through life together. Similar language is used elsewhere in the Bible to describe the greatest possible degree of closeness, such as that between a father and son, Abraham and Isaac: *"...And they went both of them together"*[7]; *"...So they went both of them together"*[8]; *"...And they rose up and went together...."*[9]

When the text uses this language to describe how Naomi and Ruth continue their journey together, it makes clear that there is absolutely no difference and no hierarchical relationship between Naomi and Ruth. This text thus emphasizes the Jewish community's obligation to accept a convert on equal footing with one born to the faith – the Torah never makes such a distinction. Moreover, the rabbis specifically forbid referring to a convert as a convert, characterizing such an act as *ona'ah*, a term associated with robbery. For by using such language, one robs or diminishes the status of the person.

Shortly after Ruth's conversion to Judaism – her spiritual marriage to God – we are given a hint that her human marriage will follow as well. As Ruth and Naomi return to the city of

---

[6] Ruth 1:19

[7] Genesis 22:6

[8] Genesis 22:8

[9] Genesis 22:19

Bethlehem, we are told that the *"whole city was astir at their arrival."*[10] Rashi explains why all the people of Bethlehem have gathered together.[11] They have come to bury the wife of Boaz, who died that very day, and they are shocked when they see Naomi, who appears embittered.

The Divine Providence that is essential and continuous in this story becomes readily apparent. Ruth enters Bethlehem as a single woman in a strange new land. Then suddenly, Boaz – who can act as her protector – becomes available to her. When you open yourself up to the Divine in the form of conversion, you open yourself up to Divine protection and other relationships as well.

I think of a young woman, Roberta, who had never married or had children. Some years ago she converted to Judaism, drawn by a deep spiritual calling. She joined a synagogue and began to participate actively in educational and social activities, including serving as a hostess for newcomers at her Sabbath table. Last year, one of her guests was a man who had recently become a widower and who now lived alone with his two children. Roberta and the widower developed an immediate rapport. "We speak so easily and effortlessly," she told me. "He has become such a dear friend." Their friendship soon blossomed into love and they recently married. Roberta was a radiant bride, and no wonder. As she describes her new life, she says, "I've married a man I love and I've acquired the family I've always dreamed of. I feel more fulfilled and complete than I ever dreamed possible."

---

[10] Ruth 1:19

[11] Rashi, Ruth 1:19

Ruth finds self-fulfillment in converting and chooses to stay with Naomi during a difficult time in Naomi's life. As Naomi and Ruth enter Bethlehem, the city's inhabitants ask, *"Is this Naomi?"*[12] Naomi looks withered and depressed. She has aged and undoubtedly lost weight. Her appearance is such that her former neighbors hardly recognize her. Moreover, she has returned without her family. The husband and sons with whom she left ten years earlier have died after a series of misfortunes, including the loss of their wealth. Naomi had been affluent, someone who traveled in covered wagons, with mules.[13] She is now poor and traveling on foot.

When the people of Bethlehem ask, *"Is this Naomi?"* it is clear that they read a great deal from her lined and weary face. For after a period of time, our face tells the entire story of our lives – it becomes the daily visual journal of our experiences. Naomi herself must recognize how her travails have affected her appearance, for she says, *"Do not call me Naomi [sweet or pleasant] but call me Mara [embittered one]...."*[14] She seems to be saying: "Change my name to reflect how I feel and look – bitter."

Naomi's inner state stems from her many hardships and losses, but also mirrors her regret at some of the life choices she has made. After all, she accompanied her husband, Elimelech, when he abandoned his friends and neighbors in Bethlehem to go to Moab where he would not be bothered to share some of his

---

12 Ruth 1:19

13 Rashi, Ruth 1:19

14 Ruth 1:20

wealth.[15] Now Naomi deeply regrets this past mistake. By speaking of her bitterness, she also acknowledges to her neighbors that she is sorry she abandoned them when they were hungry and suffering.

However, even while Naomi is confronting her inner bitterness, she extends kindness to Ruth, and Ruth reciprocates in the same manner. Kindness begets kindness. In fact, kindness as a response to pain, suffering and tragedy is one of the overriding themes of the Book of Ruth.

Kindness is crucial to the success of every relationship. Sadly, however, not all relationships are founded on kindness. I have witnessed many instances of "the shoemaker's children going barefoot." I know of psychiatrists who listen patiently to depressed patients all day long, yet have neither the interest nor the patience to support their spouses and children when they come home.

Kindness must begin at home, where it can be practiced daily. And it must characterize the dynamics of any kind of marriage, whether with God or a human being. Such is the lesson of Ruth. Her kindness and other remarkable qualities inspire us and guide us as we try to better understand what enabled her to be so special.

---

[15] Rashi, Ruth 1:1

Chapter 7

CONSCIOUSNESS

What is it about Ruth that enables her to proceed along her difficult journey? And what is it about her that causes people to notice her, think favorably of her and intervene on her behalf? One clue comes from her own words to Naomi: *"Let me go now to the field and glean among the stalks...."*[1]

Ruth is a doer. She is proactive, rather than waiting for other human beings – or even God – to intervene on her behalf. *She* decides to accompany her mother-in-law to a strange new land, people and faith. And despite her mother-in-law's protestations and good arguments in favor of her turning back, Ruth persists in her desire and accompanies Naomi on her journey back to Bethlehem. She determines and creates her own destiny.

Once in the new land, Ruth does not seem to be intimidated by the foreign culture or unfamiliar surroundings. On the contrary, she again rushes to act. She is fearless in taking her first steps in this new culture, though she cannot be certain where they will lead.

---

[1] Ruth 2:2

Ruth carries out her plan to glean. Through Divine Providence, she is directed to the field of Boaz, a nephew of Naomi's late husband, Elimelech. Boaz's very name reveals something of his character. It means "in him there is strength." Compare this description of Boaz's internal strength of character with the boastful name of Elimelech, meaning "unto me, I am a king."

Boaz is a keen judge of the character of others. He observes Ruth as she works in his field. Her demeanor and actions attract his attention and reveal Ruth's special qualities. She comes to the field early and works hard all day long, barely stopping to take a break in the hut provided for harvesters in the field. She is dressed modestly and acts that way as well, stooping down to glean the stalks of barley that have fallen on the ground.[2] She is careful not to bend over and inadvertently expose any part of her body, thereby attracting inappropriate attention from the other workers.

What Boaz perceives in Ruth is much more than her behavior. He senses her elegance, dignity and refinement of character, which combine to reveal her inner beauty. And while Ruth clearly displays traits of her noble lineage and character, she is not afraid to work hard and put her own hands into the earth.

In today's world, it is not always popular to discuss issues such as refinement and modesty. Yet the power of seduction is as strong as it has always been. I believe that many people are aware that their body language and movements can be provocative and may be misinterpreted by members of the opposite sex.

---

[2] Rashi, Ruth 2:5

Gila Manolson, the author of *The Magic Touch*,[3] frequently tells a story in her lectures about an encounter with a young friend who was getting dressed for an important job interview. The young woman fretted over the right outfit, and Gila, purposely being provocative, pulled out a revealing cocktail dress, saying, "Why not wear this?"

"Are you crazy?" the friend responded.

"Why not?" Gila pressed.

"Because if I walked into the interview wearing that, they would relate to me as a body for sale, not as a professional. They wouldn't take me seriously."

"So how do you think men relate to you when you wear this at a singles' bar?"

Startled, Gila's friend remained silent for a moment. Then she responded, admitting that her own words testified to how immodest dress is perceived, no matter what the situation. Yet, it is doubtful that the young woman would have acknowledged as much to herself the last time she had worn the revealing outfit in a social setting.

In my own professional experience, I have encountered women who consciously make use of such provocative dress. I think of one client, for example, a pleasant young woman who would come to my office on a weekly basis. During our first meeting, she was wearing a suit and appeared quite professional. However, in the weeks that followed, her style of dress changed

---

[3] Manolson, G. *The Magic Touch: A Jewish Approach to Relationships*. NY, Feldheim, 1992.

noticeably. First she began to remove her suit jacket as soon as she came in. Some weeks later, she began to "forget" to even wear the jacket. And it became apparent that she was leaving the upper buttons of her blouse unfastened, in order to reveal her cleavage.

It is not uncommon in therapeutic settings for transference to take place between a client and a therapist. An experienced physician or therapist is vigilant about looking for signs of seductive behavior and discussing them with the client or patient. Yet primal instincts are very strong, and there have been many instances of improper relationships between healers and patients. Even laws and ethical guidelines have not been able to put a stop to such behavior. And for good reason: All people, no matter how educated and socialized to cultural norms, are susceptible to the powerful primal sexual instincts that drive them.

One female client told me that she was quite conscious of her ability to stir men. In addition to dressing provocatively, she chose another way of attracting their attention. She wore many large pieces of flashy jewelry. From one of her gold necklaces hung shiny, mirror-like squares of glass. "I deliberately wear such jewelry," she told me, "so that when a man looks at me, the first thing he sees is himself reflected in my jewelry, on my body. Then I know I have him."

Ruth could have used such feminine wiles to attract a mate, perhaps one even more powerful and wealthier than Boaz, and certainly younger. But she chooses to act in accordance with her core values and her innate modesty. Those qualities extend to her speech as well. Notice how politely she speaks to the person in charge of the harvesters, though by Jewish law she has a right to glean after the harvesters have passed. She asks: *"Please allow me to glean and gather among the sheaves."* [4] Ruth is attuned to feelings – her own and those of others.

Ruth's interactions with Boaz also represent a new era in the development of male and female consciousness. As explained in a note at the end of this book,[5] Ruth's ancestor, the eldest daughter of Lot, had incestuous relations with her father that led to the birth of Moab. The description of events makes one thing clear about this episode: both of Lot's daughters knew exactly what they were doing. However, Lot, becoming intoxicated by his daughters, did not. Their plan was crystal clear in their minds, and they acted deliberately and consciously to achieve their goal – having a child by means of their father's seed in an attempt to rebuild and repopulate the world. Lot was unconscious throughout this episode, literally and figuratively. His daughters had given him wine to drink so that he was completely unaware of their comings and goings. He had no idea of the way in which he was being used.

The next stage in the development of male consciousness in the relationship between the sexes involves one of Boaz's ancestors, Judah, who was one of Jacob's sons. The Bible describes how Judah had sexual relations with Tamar, his daughter-in-law, without knowing who she was. During that encounter, Tamar was completely conscious of what she was doing. She came up with an elaborate plan, disguising herself and

---

[4] Ruth 2:7

[5] See Appendix D.

deceiving Judah into believing that she was a prostitute. But throughout this episode, Judah was unconscious of how he was being used, though he was awake and alert, unlike Lot.

When Ruth decides to go to the field and glean crops left for the poor, she shares her plan with Naomi, and Naomi gives her her blessing. *"Go, my daughter,"* [6] she tells Ruth, completely aware of what she is doing and of what may happen at Boaz's field. For she knows who Boaz is: *"And unto Naomi there was a relative on her husband's side, a man of power and substance, of the family of Elimelech, and his name was Boaz."* [7]

Though the usual term for "relative" is *karov*, here Boaz is referred to as a *moda*, from the root of the word meaning "to know." The text thus provides a very strong hint that Naomi knows exactly what she is doing. She realizes that in sending Ruth out to glean nearby, Ruth will encounter Boaz, not only a relative, but also a *"man of power and substance"* who can serve as a protector and redeemer. Naomi would not have dared send Ruth out to the field of a stranger, where she might have encountered abuse or harassment.

At this new stage in the development of consciousness between the sexes, Boaz is also completely aware of who Ruth is. Although at first he is told that she is a Moabitess, he observes how she works and how she treats others. While Ruth gleans, she is scrupulous in adhering to the laws and customs of Israel. She gathers up only the sheaves that the reapers have dropped and

---

[6] Ruth 2:2

[7] Ruth 2:1

forgotten. She does not take one sheaf more than what is designated for the poor to glean.[8] Boaz is impressed by her values – and her consistency in adhering to them – as well as by her modest demeanor.

It is Ruth's modesty and kindness that Boaz finds so attractive. He wants to protect this special woman who has come from afar and who has been so good to her mother-in-law. *"I have ordered the lads not to disturb you,"* [9] he reassures Ruth. Because she has been so scrupulous, he wants to ensure that others treat her with the respect she deserves.

Through her actions, Ruth reveals her inner qualities and true identity. Similarly, Boaz's words and actions reveal who he is. Thus, Ruth and Boaz expose their inner selves to each other, demonstrating the caring and compassion that make them so perfectly suited for one another. They are conscious of one another.

Sadly, in the family lives of most of the people I encounter, such mutual consciousness does not exist. Families often consist of people dwelling together in multiple solitudes – husband and wife, parent and child, brother and sister – each one unaware of the needs, internal realities and dreams of the other.

I think of a husband and wife who came to see me. Both were accomplished professionals who had come to California from Massachusetts. The husband was an architect who had worked on some of Boston's most innovative urban renewal projects. His

---

[8] Rashi, Ruth 2:5

[9] Ruth 2:9

wife was a professor of social work. One day, while they lived in Boston, the wife received a call that would change and disrupt both of their lives. She was offered an appointment as dean of a small liberal arts college in California. As soon as she hung up, she turned to her husband and said, "Guess what, dear? We're moving out West." Independently, she had decided to accept the position. While her husband was genuinely happy for her, he felt angered and betrayed by her instant, unilateral decision. He liked his job, his home and his friends in Boston, yet he reluctantly accompanied his wife to California. Though he eventually found suitable employment at a Los Angeles design firm, he began to feel increasingly anxious and resentful. Eventually, he sank into a severe depression.

This was clearly a marriage in which little mutual consciousness had been achieved. The wife may not have realized that one basic goal of a good liberal arts education is to achieve superior communication skills. She may have been a professor and a dean, but her interpersonal skills and ability to communicate with her husband were very limited.

By contrast, Ruth is sensitive to those around her. She demonstrates great kindness and compassion. God takes notice of Ruth and causes remarkable things to happen in her. Even when God's Name does not appear directly in the text, it is clear that Divine Providence is guiding Ruth's life. She is directed to the field of Boaz, who is to be her benefactor and protector. Boaz will now be guided to take steps that will lead to the redemption of Ruth – and ultimately, all of humankind.

Chapter 8

WELCOMING THE STRANGER

Boaz welcomes Ruth to his field in the kindest, gentlest manner possible, while at the same time watching out for her welfare and protecting her. He tells her: *"Listen well, my daughter, do not go to glean in another field, and do not go away from here, but keep close to my maidens. Keep your eyes on the field where they are harvesting, and follow them. I have ordered the lads not to disturb you; and when you are thirsty, go to the jugs and drink from the water which the lads have drawn."* [1]

Notice that during their first meeting, Boaz calls Ruth *"my daughter,"* biti, a term of endearment and closeness. Furthermore, he instructs her not to go to glean in the field of anyone else. He goes out of his way to let her know that she is welcome to stay and partake of his harvest. Boaz's actions are particularly noteworthy in light of his own circumstances at this time – he has lost his wife and has just completed observing a week of mourning for her.[2] Yet, despite his own pain and sense of loss, Boaz takes special care to welcome Ruth, thereby lessening *her* pain. No newcomer, no stranger could ask for a warmer reception in a new environment.

---

[1] Ruth 2:8–9

[2] Rashi, Ruth 1:19

Boaz's actions make me think of a couple I know who invite guests to their home every week. One person who has visited with them repeatedly told me: "It is incredible. They make me feel like I'm honoring them by coming. They beg me not to go elsewhere. I don't know what I've done to deserve it, but I feel that I've acquired some more family."

I myself have experienced such exceptional hospitality. Many years ago, when I was studying in Jerusalem, I was invited to spend a few Sabbaths with Rabbi Eliyahu Kitov and his family. On Saturday night, as I walked to the front door with Rabbi Kitov at the conclusion of the Sabbath, I prepared to express my gratitude to him. But before I could even begin to say "thank you," he turned to me and thanked *me* for having been their guest. His exceptionally kind words stay with me to this day.

Boaz extends just this kind of hospitality to Ruth, and she is deeply moved by his generosity of spirit. Even though she has already converted to Judaism, she still feels a little like a foreigner as she thanks Boaz for his kindness. She falls on her face before him, prostrating herself on the ground, and says: *"Why have I found favor in your eyes, that you should take notice of me, though I am a foreigner?"* [3]

Through her actions, however, Ruth has demonstrated that she is certainly not a foreigner to the culture and religion of Boaz. Boaz recognizes her inner qualities and seeks to protect her. He sees that she is a vulnerable woman working alone in his field, so he tells her to keep close to the other maidens who are there. And

---

[3] Ruth 2:10

he adds: *"I have ordered the lads not to disturb you."* [4] Having noticed Ruth's modest demeanor, Boaz has taken steps to ensure her safety, dignity and well-being.

The language that Boaz uses in speaking to Ruth may remind us of that found in the biblical story of Abraham. Boaz tells Ruth: *"It has been fully reported to me… how you left your father and mother and the land of your birth, and went to a people you had never known before."* [5] Notice how similar this phrasing is to that found in the Divine commandment to Abraham: *"Go forth from your country, and from the land of your birthplace, and from your father's house, to the land that I will show you."* [6] Boaz is telling Ruth that he recognizes in her a true daughter of Abraham, one who has emulated her forefather.[7]

The striking parallels between Abraham, the founder of Judaism, and Ruth, the mother of royalty, are incredible:

Abraham (Genesis 12:1)	Ruth (2:11)
go forth	you left
your father's house	your father and mother
your birthplace	the land of your birth
to the land I will show you	to a people you had never known before

---

[4] Ruth 2:9

[5] Ruth 2:11

[6] Genesis 12:1

... אֲשֶׁר־עָזַבְתְּ אָבִיךְ וְאִמֵּךְ וְאֶרֶץ מוֹלַדְתֵּךְ וַתֵּלְכִי אֶל־עַם אֲשֶׁר לֹא־יָדַעַתְּ...

לֶךְ־לְךָ מֵאַרְצְךָ וּמִמּוֹלַדְתְּךָ וּמִבֵּית אָבִיךָ אֶל־הָאָרֶץ אֲשֶׁר אַרְאֶךָּ

[7] To this day, a convert is called either a *Ben Avraham* or *Bat Avraham* (son or daughter of Abraham).

But Abraham was not the only member of his family to leave his birthplace and his family. So did his nephew, Lot. However, Lot made some poor decisions and choices, arguing with Abraham and separating himself from the good influence of his uncle. As we know, Lot's daughters then had incestuous relations with their father and engendered Moab, the ancestors of Ruth.

Now Ruth has a second chance; she has the opportunity to rectify these past wrongs. Ruth makes the right decisions in her life. A Moabitess by birth, she chooses to return to Bethlehem with her mother-in-law. She converts to the religion of Abraham. She becomes the forebear of the Messiah. Clearly, biology is not destiny.

To undertake the journey of an Abraham or a Ruth is to confront many fears. It is difficult – and for many, impossible – to let go of the connections to one's home and one's past. As Heinz Kohut brilliantly demonstrated in his theory of object relations,[8] most people are connected to objects, even the most temporary possessions of life. One highly intelligent woman I know confessed that even years after the 1994 Northridge earthquake, she cannot get over the loss of her dinnerware set, which she has been unable to replace.

Her feelings are certainly normal and understandable. People hold onto objects for a feeling of security in the face of the great insecurity of the human condition. I regularly see many examples

---

[8] Kohut, H. *The Analysis of the Self.* NY: International Universities Press, 1971.

of this phenomenon. One man in particular, Mitchell, comes to mind. A young widower, he immigrated to Los Angeles from London several years ago after the death of his wife. He established himself professionally and personally and was quite content in Los Angeles, but he continued to pay rent on his furnished London apartment. In his heart, he was not sure where his home really was. He visited London frequently. Then, last year he was introduced by mutual friends to a lovely young woman. They hit it off immediately and started spending all of their free time together. Soon, they could not imagine being apart, and they decided to marry. Only after they wed was Mitchell truly ready to begin anew, severing his ties with the objects of his past. He finally let go of his London apartment and sold all of its contents to the incoming tenant. His love and commitment to another human being provided him with all the security he needed to move on.

Attachment to objects – to the good life – can hold us back. Only those whose primary attachment and connection is with God will find the courage to set out on the journey of Abraham and Ruth.

One young man I know is a model of rising to that challenge. Born into a wealthy family that is prominent in the entertainment industry, he was groomed his entire life to become a movie producer. His parents offered him everything – money, power, contacts and connections. Yet he felt spiritually unfulfilled in the film world. He decided to enter rabbinical school and pursue what seemed most important and meaningful to him. By choosing this road less traveled, he exposed himself to the criticism and ridicule of his family and friends. Yet he persevered and found fulfillment in his own way. He undertook the journey of Abraham and Ruth.

Any person who would undertake such a difficult, dangerous and frightening journey requires special Divine protection. That is what was promised to Abraham when he became the first convert to Judaism, leaving the home and land of his father, Terach, an idol-worshipper. Similarly, Boaz prays that the God of Israel will protect Ruth, a new convert, and reward her for her deeds. When Boaz first encounters Ruth in his field, he blesses her as follows: *"May the Lord reward your deed, may you be given full recompense from the Lord, God of Israel, for you have come to seek refuge under His wings."* [9] The image of a mother bird spreading her wings to shelter her young is a gentle, love-filled metaphor, and it is the very formulation that is used today to welcome converts into the people of Israel, *"under the [sheltering] wings of the Divine Presence."* [10]

Boaz's words touch Ruth's heart and soul. She tells him, *"You have comforted me, and have spoken to the heart of your handmaid...."* [11] She accepts Boaz's generous offer of hospitality, sitting beside the harvesters in his field and eating the roasted grain that he offers her. She leaves some food uneaten,[12] intending to take it home to share with her mother-in-law, Naomi. In this way, Ruth takes advantage of an opportunity to repair the past – she demonstrates how different she is from her selfish Moabite forebears, who

---

[9] Ruth 2:12

[10] Maimonides. *Mishneh Torah. Hilkhot Gerut* 13:1

[11] Ruth 2:13

[12] Ruth 2:14

74

wanted to sell bread and water to the Israelites wandering through the desert. By contrast, she is generous, empathic and giving. Her kindness is the same sort of kindness that was the hallmark of Abraham.

Like Ruth, Boaz is also kind and modest. Even as he takes steps to protect and help Ruth, he does so discreetly. For example, Boaz orders his young men: *"Let her glean even among the sheaves, and do not humiliate her. Let some sheaves fall for her even from the bundles, and leave them for her to glean, and do not rebuke her."* [13]

Boaz's behavior reminds me of a physician I know, a humble man who is a true healer. Over the past twenty years, I have seen, time and again, how he has created good in the lives of those around him. I have observed the way he treats his employees, from his laboratory assistant to his secretary to his gardener. He makes sure to pay them in a generous and timely fashion, while treating them with respect and dignity. When his gardener's daughter recently needed knee surgery, he made sure that the girl received the best possible care at the hospital where he practices. The gardener had no insurance to cover the procedure, so this physician arranged with his colleagues to donate their services. The gardener was told that all of the medical care had been provided through the free services of Los Angeles County, to which he was entitled. In ensuring that the father retained his dignity, and in acting so discreetly, this physician was following in the footsteps of Boaz.

---

[13] Ruth 2:15–16

The world that Ruth and Boaz inhabited is much the same as our own. We live in a society where competition, jealousy and trying to keep up with our neighbors are the norm. People are often uncaring. It is routine in the medical world that some physicians spend only seconds – not even minutes – in patients' rooms. However, there are those who do take the time to answer questions completely, offer comfort and provide guidance and advice. They may lose a little bit of money in these extended encounters, but think of what they – and the world – gain from this compassionate use of their time. Imagine a society in which such behavior was the norm. It is such a society that all people are called upon to create, and the models presented in the story of Ruth show us the way.

When Boaz provides emotional, physical and financial support for Ruth, while recognizing and respecting the unique journey of her life, he emulates the ways of the Almighty. He demonstrates that Ruth will be sheltered not only under the Divine wings, but also in his own loving embrace.

Boaz's constant and consistent demonstrations of kindness, compassion and sensitivity demonstrate what a fitting partner he will be for Ruth, his kindred spirit. He will also be the ideal son-in-law for Naomi, herself a model of kindness and a source of blessings.

Chapter 9

FOOD FOR THE SOUL

When Ruth goes to Boaz's field, she works hard to gather food for herself and Naomi: *"So she gleaned in the field until evening and she milled that which she gleaned, and produced about an ephah of barley. She carried it and went into the city. Her mother-in-law saw what she had gleaned, and she took it out and she gave her what she had left over after eating her fill."* [1]

We can see that Ruth deals with food quite differently from how most of us do today. We live in a food-obsessed culture. Only in today's world do we witness the phenomenon of a man suing a hamburger chain for serving fatty foods that "made" him obese! Only today are so many young women dying from anorexia or suffering from bulimia, an eating disorder characterized by eating to excess and then vomiting one's meal. Only today do millions of people go to bed hungry and malnourished while millions of others monitor their grams of food intake, hoping against hope to lose weight or at least not to gain another ounce.

While the extremes of eating behaviors and disorders might be more readily apparent today than ever before, the relationship

---

[1] Ruth 2:17–18

between humans and what they eat has really not changed very much. A basic animal drive – hunger – has always led humans to search for and consume food. But how they eat, with whom they eat, and how much they eat depends on many factors. Hunger is more than just a physical drive. It has a strong emotional component as well. While food is basic to life, eating is a complex activity.

As we have seen, the Book of Ruth opens with a scene of famine. Famine is fairly difficult for those of us in the developed world to comprehend. It is hard for us to empathize with people facing all-consuming hunger, having little or nothing to eat or drink.

During a famine, every day, every waking moment, becomes a challenge of sheer endurance. Hunger hurts. It gnaws at people's bellies and brains, forcing them to focus all of their attention on what they lack. They cannot think lofty thoughts. They cannot think of anything other than their hunger. They cannot and do not think about anyone beyond themselves, even members of their own family. As inconceivable as it might seem, mothers might even turn on their children. People will do anything to survive. They cannot plan for the future or even dream of it. Their fatigue and weak limbs prevent them from walking even a short distance to search for something to sustain themselves. Many will die. Many will lack the will to go on.

The famine described in the first verse of the Book of Ruth refers to more than the absence of produce in the fields. The picture we get is of a land and a people and a family that are spiritually and physically hungry. Elimelech, rich enough to sustain his entire community, leads his family far away from their home in Bethlehem to the land of Moab so that he will not have to share his wealth – and abundant stores of food – with neighbors or strangers, with anyone who might be in need.

What kind of person can be so callous and insensitive to the needs of others?

Unfortunately, Elimelech was and is not unique. I recently saw a man get out of his shiny new car and obtain a parking ticket from a valet while ignoring a homeless man on the pavement as he entered the lobby of an exclusive hotel to attend a sumptuous banquet.

Perhaps we all need to be reminded that we are not the sources of our own wealth. Man is not the ultimate cultivator and harvester of food. Man does not determine where and when crops will flourish, when rain and wind and soil conditions will promote growth rather than stifle it. Throughout the Bible, we are often asked to take note of the relationship between human behavior and God's actions, i.e., the forces of nature. We are clearly reminded of this reality when we learn about Naomi's decision to return from Moab to Bethlehem, *"for she had heard in the fields of Moab that God had cared for His people to give them food."* [2] Divine Providence and intercession have once again made it possible for farmers in Bethlehem to sow, harvest and reap crops. By the time Naomi and Ruth return to Bethlehem, it is *"the start of the barley harvest."* [3]

---

[2] Ruth 1:6

[3] Ruth 1:22

So Bethlehem is described both as a place of famine and later, as a place of harvest. The same location can be both, depending on the people who reside there and the way they behave and interact. I once heard a story that demonstrates just this point:

A villager wanted to know what hell looked like and dispatched an angel to explore and describe it. The angel returned and said: "Hell is a terrible place, where people face the most awful torture and deprivation. Everyone there has rigid arms that cannot bend at the elbow. Thus, at every meal, when food is set before them, they cry out in hunger but they cannot raise the food from their plates to their mouths."

"Well," said the villager, "that is a most frightening description. Now go up to heaven and see what it is like."

A short time later, the angel returned with a glowing report. "Heaven is a wonderful place," he said.

"What is it like?" asked the villager.

"Well, first of all, the people there all have rigid arms that do not bend at the elbow," replied the angel.

"But I don't understand. That is exactly how you described hell."

"Yes, but there is one important difference. In heaven, the diners sit next to one another. Each one raises a forkful of food in his rigid arm so that his neighbor can then eat. Then the neighbor reciprocates in kind. That is the only difference between heaven and hell."

When Ruth and Naomi return to Bethlehem, it is not at all the same as when Elimelech left it. It is clear that the society that Ruth and Naomi encounter on their return to Bethlehem is no longer characterized by greed and selfishness. The harvesters in Boaz's field readily and happily allow Ruth to glean from what they leave behind. Boaz even tells his workers to purposely let some extra grain fall so that Ruth can gather more: *"Let some sheaves fall for her even from the bundles, and leave them for her to glean, and do not rebuke her."* [4] Ruth works hard, gathering as much barley as she can. Yet, she is careful not to take more than what she is legally entitled to gather,[5] and does not keep all the food for herself, but shares it with her mother-in-law.

In another act of kindness, Boaz invites Ruth to share in the meal of the workers.[6] Eating with a group elevates and enriches both the act and the soul. It is interesting to note how animals go off to eat in separate corners, each one devouring as much as possible for himself. By contrast, when humans come together for a meal, they create a social occasion. What is ingested is more than food. Participants are nourished by conversation, caring and perhaps singing. In such a gathering, God dwells as well. At the end of such a meal, the spirit of community that has pervaded it allows the group to recite grace together.

By contrast, a solitary hunter heads off into his own terrain, constantly looking back over his shoulder to make sure that no pursuer – animal or human – is stalking him. He quickly tears at whatever food he finds or kills, trying to get it down before some predator can snatch it away. He is anxious and stressed, and

---

[4] Ruth 2:16

[5] Rashi, Ruth 2:5

[6] Ruth 2:14

adrenaline rushes through his system. He may be ingesting food, but he is not enjoying a meal.

When we eat or drink alone, uninhibited by social conventions, we tend to only our most basic, animal needs. We may overindulge more than we would in a social setting. Perhaps that is why those who seek intervention for addiction to alcohol or food are often asked, "Do you drink (or eat) alone? Do you hide your drink (or food)?" One client who responded "yes" to those questions told me, "I don't do alcohol. I do food."

By contrast, Ruth demonstrates a balanced approach to life and to food. As she sits besides the harvesters, Boaz hands her some roasted grain. It is here that we see just how healthy a relationship Ruth has with food and how different she is from her late father-in-law, Elimelech. She makes use of this second chance to rectify what Elimelech did in the past: *"… She ate and was satisfied, and **left some over.**"* [7]

Ruth knows that it takes only a moderate amount of food to sustain her. Anything else is unnecessary excess. She has discovered "portion control" long before it has become widely known! She also realizes that if she takes more than what she truly needs, she will have less to share with Naomi and others who may need it. And so, Ruth's righteousness is reflected, in part, in how she gleans – taking only what is due her and not more, and how she eats – always sharing with others.

It takes much less to nourish ourselves than we think. One physician I know suggests that many digestive problems can be

---

[7] Ruth 2:14

prevented or alleviated if we just give thought to "anything and everything we put in our mouth." Will it nourish us? Will it enhance our health? Do we really need it – now?

Ruth's ability to feel satiated is noteworthy. It is quite common for people to gorge themselves at food-laden tables without ever feeling satisfied. That is because their hunger is more than physical. They may feel full, but not satiated. I recently heard a physician describe the typical mid-afternoon cravings that descend on many people at around 4:00 P.M. He said that only part of this phenomenon could be attributed to blood-sugar levels and insulin production. The rest of this need is purely emotional and it, too, needs to be nurtured.

Ruth and Naomi nurture their bodies and their spirits when they sit down to enjoy a meal prepared from the grain that Ruth has gleaned in Boaz's field, for this food was gathered and prepared with love, the most important ingredient in a wholesome and satisfying meal. A spoonful of love makes the food go down in the most delightful – and healthy – way.

Furthermore, the way in which Ruth, Naomi and Boaz relate to food provides insight into their values and characters. Their disciplined approach to eating indicates that they are capable of setting boundaries in every aspect of their behavior, including their sexuality.

Part III: SEXUALITY

The Book of Ruth (Summary of Chapter 3)

Naomi expresses her concern for Ruth's future security. She directs Ruth to wash, perfume and dress herself and then to go down to Boaz's threshing-floor at night. There Ruth is to notice where Boaz beds down after he eats and drinks. Then she is to uncover his feet, lie down and wait for Boaz to tell her what to do. At midnight, Boaz awakens and discovers Ruth at his feet. Ruth asks him to "spread your mantle over your handmaid, for you are a near kinsman [first cousin]." In effect, she is asking Boaz to marry her. Boaz praises Ruth for turning to him rather than pursuing younger men. He promises to do as Ruth asks if a closer relative [uncle] does not choose to claim her. He tells her to stay the night and leave early in the morning before anyone could recognize her. Sending her away before the sun comes up, he gives her a large amount of grain as a gift for Naomi. Ruth tells Naomi what happened, and Naomi reassures her that Boaz will hasten to take care of the relationship that very day.

Chapter 10

A TEST AT MIDNIGHT

"Naomi, her mother-in-law, said to her, 'My daughter, I shall seek security for you, which will be good for you. Now, Boaz, our kinsman, with whose maidens you have been, he will be winnowing the barley on the threshing-floor tonight. And you shall bathe and scent yourself, dress yourself in your finest garb, and go down to the threshing-floor....' " [1]

With these words, Naomi sends Ruth out on a mission that will change their lives. Naomi is very aware of Ruth's vulnerability as a foreigner and as a single woman. So Naomi takes steps to protect Ruth as best as she can, while continuing to show great kindness and consideration towards her daughter-in-law. Once again, Naomi calls Ruth *"biti,"* my daughter.[2] By using this term of endearment, Naomi is showing respect both to Ruth and to her late son, Machlon, who was married to Ruth.

Naomi seems anxious to have Ruth enjoy the security that comes with marriage. It is clear that as a single woman, Ruth did not enjoy much of an independent identity or many benefits. Lest we think that this situation was limited to Bethlehem thousands of

---

[1] Ruth 3:1–3

[2] Ruth 3:1

years ago, we have only to look around the world today to find that the situation of the single woman has not changed very much.

I recently read a report about a single woman in Nigeria, Amina Lawal, who was sentenced to death by stoning for having a child out of wedlock. Only through the intervention of people around the world and Amnesty International was she spared the death penalty. Similarly, recent reports from India confirm that many widows and divorcees in that country are often reduced to begging or subsisting in other ways on the margins of society. One Indian man living in the United States told me that he had wanted to divorce his wife back in India, but did not because he had compassion for her. He realized that were she divorced and alone, she would become a nonentity.

Even in Los Angeles, many women tell me that they have experienced similar discrimination, even though their livelihoods and physical survival have not necessarily been at stake. One woman who has experienced divorce told me that after the change in her marital status, "I became invisible." She went on to describe her disappointment in communal institutions for not providing inclusive social opportunities for single people.

Another woman, whose parents divorced many years ago, described how her mother had difficulty establishing credit in her own name. And a widow sadly recounted to me how after her husband's death, her entire social circle disappeared. He had been a prominent physician in the community and she was always at his side, but when he was no longer around, his fellow physicians forgot about her. Their behavior reflected, in part, their feeling that she had no identity of her own. It also reflected a widespread fear – in social gatherings of couples, a suddenly single woman is often seen as a threat, a potential temptress who might threaten the marriages of others.

As a widow, Naomi is aware of her own vulnerability and that of her beloved daughter-in-law. Recognizing the need to provide security and comfort for Ruth, Naomi sets a daring plan in motion. She will send Ruth down to Boaz's threshing-floor in the middle of the night to speak to Boaz face-to-face and heart-to-heart in order to learn if he will marry her.

How can Naomi take this great chance? How can she be certain of how Ruth and Boaz will behave under these circumstances? The truth is, of course, that Naomi cannot be certain of anything. No one can predict human behavior, particularly in the realm of sexuality.

I suggest that Naomi's intention was to set up for Ruth and Boaz the opportunity – the second chance – to rectify ancient mistakes. As we have seen, their family origins can be traced to incest (Lot and his daughters) and sexual deception (Tamar and Judah). Now Ruth, a direct descendent of Lot and his eldest daughter, and Boaz, a direct descendent of Tamar and her father-in-law, Judah, can *repair* the actions of their ancestors and, consequently, of the collective Israelite people.

Naomi is in a unique position to be the intermediary between Ruth and Boaz since she is related to both of them. She is aware of certain truths that lead her to hope for and anticipate the best. As she describes her plan to Ruth, Naomi refers to Boaz as *"modatanu,"*[3] not just a kinsman but someone who is "known to us." As mentioned in chapter 7, the text also used this language earlier to describe Boaz.[4] Naomi knows a great deal about this relative of hers. She has heard how kindly he dealt with Ruth while she gleaned in his field: He offered her food and drink, he worried about her personal safety and assured her, *"I have ordered the lads not to disturb you."*[5] Naomi now reminds Ruth of Boaz's impeccable behavior.[6] Clearly, he is a person of high moral character.

Naomi is also aware of Boaz's other attributes. He puts on no airs and is responsible and reliable. For example, as she tells Ruth, *"Now Boaz, our kinsman… will be winnowing the barley on the threshing-floor tonight."*[7] Boaz was a nobleman, a prince, yet he took it upon himself to personally guard his field and his crops.

I am struck by the tremendous insights into human nature that can be found in the Bible. On the phrase, *"he will be winnowing… tonight,"* Rashi comments, "Because the generation was unrestrained in theft and robbery; he would sleep in his granary to guard his granary." How strange – and how sad – that as we read this verse several thousand years later, we understand and identify with Boaz's concerns about potential theft.

---

[3] Ruth 3:2

[4] Ruth 2:1

[5] Ruth 2:9

[6] Ruth 3:2

[7] Ruth 3:2

Boaz will be alone and vulnerable as he guards his harvest. Naomi gives Ruth very explicit instructions about how to prepare herself for her encounter with him. She is to bathe, anoint and clothe herself in a way that reflects her purity, spirituality and values.

Of course, what will actually transpire at the threshing-floor is a great unknown, and Naomi's plan and specific instructions carry risks. There is no way that she or anyone else can predict the behavior of Ruth *or* Boaz. But there are certain truths of which Naomi is aware, and by her very language she imparts crucial lessons to Ruth.

In this episode, some of Naomi's words are literally spelled one way in the text, but read in another, so that they simultaneously convey two messages to Ruth and to the reader of the text. Throughout the Book of Ruth, there are numerous instances of variance between the written Hebrew text and the way the text is traditionally read. That is to say, while a specific spelling appears in the actual printed text, a variant reading guides the reader to pronounce and understand a particular word or phrase in a slightly different manner. For example, the text directs us to read and understand that Naomi told Ruth, *"you go down [ve-yaradt]"* [8] to the threshing-floor, while the actual written text reads *"ve-yaradeti"* – I will go down. Thus, two simultaneous messages are conveyed to us, just as they were to Ruth: "Go down, but I will be with you. I will go down there as well. I will accompany you on this grand mission that you are undertaking." The subliminal message in the

---

[8] Ruth 3:3

text is that Naomi is hinting that she herself would be willing to undertake everything she is suggesting to Ruth. "I would not hesitate for an instant to do what I am asking of you," she is telling Ruth. Naomi is making it as clear as possible that she will accompany Ruth, perhaps not physically but definitely psychically.

Naomi is aware of the power of her psychic presence. She hopes that by "going down" to the threshing-floor with Ruth, she will be able to guide Ruth to do the right thing. She also has great confidence in Ruth. After all, Ruth has left her mother, her father and her homeland to join a new nation and a new religion. Her actions were not undertaken lightly. Her purpose was and remains serious. Naomi assumes that when Ruth goes down to the threshing-floor, it will likewise be for a serious and holy purpose.

Naomi also knows something about Boaz. She feels sure that Boaz is a man to be trusted, even at night, even while he lies alone on his threshing-floor. Naomi further realizes that Ruth has already spent quite a bit of time in the company of Boaz, while gathering sheaves in his field, and Boaz has not proposed marriage. So she decides to take the initiative on behalf of Ruth.

In doing so, Naomi demonstrates her wisdom and knowledge of human nature. *"Do not identify yourself to the man until he has finished eating and drinking."* [9] First make sure that his hunger is satiated before turning his mind to other thoughts. Naomi further instructs Ruth to note where Boaz sleeps, uncover his feet and lie down next to him. By uncovering only his feet, Ruth will not be

---

[9] Ruth 3:3

too seductive. She will not touch any other part of his body, such as his face, that might arouse him and lead to sexual relations.

It is Ruth's actions that propel this story forward. She listens to Naomi, dressing and acting according to her mother-in-law's instructions, and goes down to the threshing-floor as she has been told to do. Naomi is busily working behind the scenes, orchestrating the encounters and experiences of those nearest and dearest to her.

Together, Naomi and Ruth make use of this opportunity to correct the past. Their choices are very different from those of Lot's daughters, who tricked their father into having incestuous relations with them in order to perpetuate their lineage.

In our story, Naomi is clearly steering Ruth towards a man who will not only protect her, but will also allow her to fulfill the sacred roles of wife and mother. As Ruth obeys her mother-in-law, she once again demonstrates that she has converted with all her heart. To Naomi's instructions, she replies: *"All that you say to me, I will do,"* [10] using language that is virtually identical to that of the Israelites at the time of their mass conversion, their acceptance of the Torah at Mount Sinai: *"All the Lord has spoken, we will do."* [11]

Ruth's fine character is revealed again at this time. Just as her dress and demeanor made her stand out from the other maidens when she was gleaning in Boaz's field, she independently decides to reverse the order of Naomi's instructions to her. She *first* goes down to where Boaz is spending the night, and only *then* does she

---

[10] Ruth 3:5

[11] Exodus 19:8

dress and anoint herself. She fears that if she is seen going down to the threshing-floor adorned in her finest, she might be perceived as a woman out to seduce a man. She does not want to initiate an encounter like the one between Tamar and Judah. She recognizes the opportunity of this second chance to rectify the past and she acts on it.

Similarly, when the time finally comes for Ruth to reveal herself to Boaz,[12] she will remind him of his family's role and responsibility. She will not seduce him and then explain her intentions. Ruth uses this second chance to "undo" the actions of Lot's daughters and of Tamar. She interacts with Boaz in an appropriate way, with modesty and honesty. If Boaz acts as Naomi hopes, he will become a redeemer not only for Ruth, but also for Naomi herself. But before that can happen, Boaz and Ruth need to meet under very strange circumstances and share an intimate conversation in the middle of the night.

[12] Ruth 3:9

Chapter 11

CONVERSATIONS IN THE NIGHT

"So she [Ruth] went down to the threshing-floor, and did exactly as her mother-in-law had bidden her." [1]

Naomi has set up quite an experiment, quite a test for her daughter-in-law and for Boaz. Naomi hopes and prays that her plan will proceed smoothly and that Ruth and Boaz will behave honorably.

And they do. Both Boaz and Ruth rise to the occasion and make the most of this opportunity to rectify their ancestors' past behavior. Down on the threshing-floor, Ruth follows Naomi's instructions. She observes as Boaz eats and drinks, and notes where he lies down to sleep, at the end of the grain pile.[2] She approaches him quietly, and uncovers his feet by lifting his blanket. When his feet become cold, he will wake up. This forward behavior is quite uncharacteristic of modest Ruth and it must not be easy for her. Why does Naomi demand this of her instead of devising another way of approaching Boaz? Why does she not

---

[1] Ruth 3:6

[2] Ruth 3:7

speak on Ruth's behalf for example, once she discerns Boaz's interest in the young woman?

Perhaps one reason that Naomi sets up such a challenging encounter for Ruth is that she knows that converts usually have to prove themselves as legitimate members of their new communities. Others are observing them, watching for any missteps or backsliding. Naomi realizes that for Ruth to be completely, wholeheartedly accepted into the Israelite fold, she will have to demonstrate that she is *more* than good enough, that she possesses the highest morals and finest character that anyone could imagine. Naomi therefore creates a scenario in which Ruth can demonstrate her true nobility of character.

The forbidden elements of both the Lot and Judah stories do not happen here. The Tamar-Judah scenario could have been repeated by Ruth and Boaz on the threshing-floor – but it does not occur. As a result, the Ruth-Boaz episode has a *redemptive* quality. Furthermore, we are shown a much more refined approach to dealing with a particular set of circumstances. Ruth and Boaz demonstrate that redemption can be brought about through ethical, legitimate means. And as a result of their approach to the problem, they and their descendents are blessed.

When Ruth uncovers Boaz's feet and he is startled awake, he asks her: *"Who are you?"*[3] Boaz actually recognizes Ruth, but is mystified by her behavior, which is so unlike anything he has observed from her before. Boaz seems to be saying: "I don't

---

[3] Ruth 3:9

understand what you are doing. It's not within the range of anything I've ever experienced before from you."

However, in a living relationship, many things become possible as part of the adventure of one's own life and that of another. Ruth's atypical behavior extends to more than lying at Boaz's feet in a secluded place in the middle of the night. When Boaz awakens and asks who is next to him, Ruth responds: *"I am Ruth, your handmaid: spread your mantle over your handmaid, for you are a near kinsman."* [4] With these words, Ruth is, in fact, asking Boaz to marry her. She is being quite direct and forward. When she invokes the image of Boaz spreading his garment over her, she is alluding to the marriage ceremony. To this day, in some Jewish traditions, the groom spreads the *tallit* – the prayer shawl – above his head and that of his bride and then wraps them both in it. In so doing he is spreading his four-cornered, fringed garment over them both. In other Jewish traditions, the prayer shawl is sometimes used as a *chuppah* – the marriage canopy – under which the bride and groom stand together to be joined in matrimony.

Ruth's nighttime encounter with Boaz at the threshing-floor illustrates two important factors in the success of Ruth's journey: First, Ruth takes the initiative. She is not passive, but active – first in cleaving to Naomi and initiating her conversion, and then in going to the threshing-floor and initiating a marriage proposal to Boaz. Second, the order in which events occur is most significant, reflecting Ruth's process of development. Her first "marriage" is with God, through her conversion process. Only then can her

---

[4] Ruth 3:9

second marriage take place with Boaz, a human being. This sequence is crucial to the success of any relationship.

For anyone, the most important goal of all is to develop a *living* relationship with God. While this is certainly a challenging process, achieving such a relationship allows one to speak more freely, to feel greater inner conviction and strength, and to be more empowered than ever before. One example of someone who achieved this goal is Etty Hillesum, a 29-year-old Dutch Jew who spent the last months of her life in Westerbork, a transit camp in the Netherlands for those being deported to Auschwitz. There, she nursed the sick in the hospital barracks and wrote in her diary about her spontaneous need for prayer:[5] "…Time and again it sours straight from my heart – I can't help it, that's just the way it is, like some elementary force – the feeling that life is glorious and magnificent…."

In another entry, written several months before her death, she wrote:[6] "You have made me so rich, oh God, please let me share Your beauty with open hands. My life has become an uninterrupted dialogue with You, Oh God, one great dialogue. Sometimes when I stand in some corner of the camp, my feet planted on Your earth, my eyes raised towards Your Heaven, tears run down my face, tears of deep emotion and gratitude. At night, too, when I lie in my bed and rest in You, Oh God, tears of

---

[5] Hillesum, Etty. *An Interrupted Life: The Diaries of Etty Hillesum, 1941–43*. NY: Pocket Books, 1985, p. 247.

[6] Hillesum, Etty. *Letters from Westerbork*. NY: Pantheon Books, 1986, p. 116.

gratitude run down my face, and that is my prayer.... My life is one great dialogue with You."

In any relationship, with the Divine or with another human being, it is important to keep on talking, even if the relationship becomes challenging. It is also vital not to block out strange or aberrant behavior in the other, but rather to make that behavior part of the composite picture. This is necessarily a slow, difficult and powerful process. *Such a relationship does not remain static.* There are seasons to it.

Furthermore, *every relationship requires commitment* in order for it to succeed. One commits to the relationship, not just a person. For example, Ruth commits to Naomi, and then further commits to Judaism. Ruth accomplishes many changes in her life in a brief span of time. As always, the presence of one – just one loving person in someone's life – enables many things. For Ruth, Naomi is that person.

Ruth's behavior further demonstrates that although there is such a thing as destiny, we have to be proactive. We may not know which path to choose, yet we are endowed with free choice. Sometimes one choice on one day, in one moment, can change the course of your life and the lives of others. Such is the day of a marriage.

When Ruth proposes marriage, she has certain goals in mind: protection, security and children. Boaz is receptive to Ruth's proposal. He speaks to her gently: *"Your latest act of kindness has exceeded your earlier kindness, since you did not go after the younger men, whether poor or rich."* [7]

When Boaz speaks of Ruth's "latest act of kindness," he is referring to her choosing him, an old man, over potential younger suitors. His words also bring to mind Ruth's prior act of kindness – to her mother-in-law, Naomi, from whom she refused to part. Boaz may be reminding Ruth: "You likewise did not abandon Naomi, and she is also elderly."

Under a blanket, anything is possible. People can speak heart to heart. However, even though Ruth and Boaz desire each other, they exercise great restraint when it comes to acting on their feelings.

---

[7] Ruth 3:10

Chapter 12

IS SEXUAL RESTRAINT EVER POSSIBLE BETWEEN
A MAN AND A WOMAN?

Boaz and Ruth have a lot to teach us during their first private meeting, which takes place at night, on a secluded threshing-floor. Some of these lessons may be learned from their words, while others are apparent from their behavior.

Boaz's first words to Ruth are truly instructive, a master class in communication. He tells Ruth, *"Now, though it is true that I am a near kinsman, yet there is a kinsman who is even closer than I."* [1] This is the way that the verse is traditionally read. However, the written version of the text actually includes one additional word – *im*, meaning "if." The "if" is there, but Boaz has not articulated it. He has *not* said, "*If* I am a near kinsman…." Thus his statement makes clear that his support for Ruth is unconditional.

From Boaz's words, we can deduce that any reservations – if one harbors them at all – should not be mentioned or should certainly not be mentioned at the outset, before one has had a chance to say anything positive. Had Boaz said "if," he might have

---

[1] Ruth 3:12

indicated to Ruth that, "maybe I'm not available to redeem you." People tend to hear "if" as "yes, but."

Boaz teaches us the importance of choosing our words wisely. For example, while it is good to be truthful, beware of those who say, "Can I be totally honest with you?" First, the nature of communication precludes that as a possibility. Second, an attempt at total honesty can ruin a relationship. Third, in some circumstances, such as in the practice of medicine, truth-telling can even be destructive.

Several cases come quickly to mind. A few years ago, one of the doctors on staff at a hospital, a psychiatrist, was diagnosed with a terminal illness. His attending physician felt that it would not be in Dr. Mark's best interest to know how much time he had left to live. But Dr. Mark persisted, saying, "I'm a psychiatrist. I can handle any news you're going to give me. I want the whole truth, and I want it now." So his physician told him: "You know you've got cancer, and it's stage 4. I don't think you've got more than six or seven months left." Dr. Mark thought he assimilated all this information well and that he could grasp it intellectually. Yet he was wrong. Soon after hearing this news, he went into a severe depression. Soon after that, he died.

Another patient, not a physician, told me that she was shocked beyond words at the way her surgeon communicated with her. "You won't believe what he said to me as I was coming out of anesthesia after surgery," she told me. "His first words to me were, 'The tumor was inoperable.' Can you believe that? If he had just presented his findings at the right time, in the right place, after some words of encouragement, I wouldn't have lost hope."

The insensitivity of some people is truly astonishing. One woman told me that she and her husband had consulted a cardiologist about her husband's worsening heart condition. At one point, the doctor asked the husband to leave the room and then said to the wife, "What do you think I can do for a dying man?" There had to be a thousand other ways to tell her the truth – that there was no treatment available for this terminally ill man – yet this doctor chose the cruelest way possible.

Boaz, however, knows what to say and when to say it. His words to Ruth illustrate his fine character, sensitivity and compassion: *"And now, my daughter, fear not; whatever you ask, I will do for you, for it is known to all who sit in the gate of my people that you are a virtuous woman. Now, though it is true that I am a near kinsman, yet there is a kinsman who is even closer than I."* [2]

In effect he is telling her, "I will redeem you. I will be there for you. Let us explore the options, including the fact that there seems to be a relative who is closer to you than I am." The closer relative to whom he is referring is Elimelech's brother, Tov,[3] meaning "Good," who is also referred to as *Ploni Almoni*, a name like "John Doe."

Some of Boaz's words to Ruth are puzzling. "… *Stay the night… lie here until the morning,"* [4] he tells her. What does he mean by this? Why would he put himself and Ruth in such a delicate, potentially compromising situation?

---

[2] Ruth 3:11–12

[3] Ruth 3:13

[4] Ruth 3:13

I believe that Ruth and Boaz are setting an example for the rest of the world, for all times and all places. When it comes to issues of sexuality, restraint is certainly not the norm – it is the exception. People are quick to give into temptation as they try to escape loneliness and boredom, and as they reach out longingly for a touch, an embrace and a moment of pleasure. When they act in this way, they may feel good for a moment but soon, often the next morning, they feel worse. They feel even lonelier and guilt-ridden, and they develop lower self-esteem. They are left with a sense of confusion and emptiness. "What did I do?" they wonder. And such behavior tends easily to get out of hand, such as in the case of drug addiction. At first, it takes only a small amount of a substance or activity to achieve a "high." But with repeated exposure, a larger and larger dose is required to achieve that state.

Boaz and Ruth do not seek an easy "fix," a quick way to feel good. They demonstrate that the path to redemption includes putting God at the center of the most intimate human relationships. Boaz and Ruth each know what can happen when this does not occur. Each of them possesses what Jungian psychology refers to as a "collective unconscious" of their pasts. Boaz knows that he is descended from Tamar's deceptive liaison with Judah. Ruth understands all too well that as a Moabitess, her lineage can be traced back to the incestuous relationship between Lot and his daughters.

But Ruth and Boaz understand how to make positive use of this chance they have been offered. Consequently, the moment when Ruth lies next to Boaz at the threshing-floor becomes a turning point in the history of this couple and this people. Ruth and Boaz confront a pivotal moment in their relationship. They understand how their present actions can rectify their pasts in order to bring about a different, hopeful future. They demonstrate how all people, no matter who their ancestors are, and no matter what they have done in their pasts, can create new beginnings and new memories.

This message of vision and hope is one that we need to hear. We are used to a different reality, one in which an alcoholic or abuser repeats the unhealthy patterns of a parent. Even patterns of incest and sexual manipulation are likely to recur. Yet, the implication here is that restraint is always possible, even though it may be difficult.

The key to Boaz's successful struggle with himself is what he says and does after he asks Ruth to stay the night and promises to redeem her: *"… as God lives, lie here until the morning."* [5] This is Boaz's oath. When he acknowledges that "God is alive" inside his inner being, he finds the strength necessary to resist temptation.

Boaz's oath to the living God is central to our story. It embodies a promise, directed to Ruth, that nothing improper will happen between them. And Ruth promises to honor that commitment. The recognition of a living God is what allows Boaz to make the right choices and to create a new beginning for his family and his people.

We, too, can start over again and take advantage of second chances and new beginnings that are offered to us. In order to utilize these wonderful gifts, we need only recognize and accept

---

[5] Ruth 3:13

the living presence of God in our lives. What do I mean by that? Simply put, that no matter who we are, no matter where we are, no matter what we are doing, we can sense God's presence. That presence can become as real to us as the road we walk on and the wind that blows through our hair. We have only to be attuned to it, to listen and to feel it in every step we take.

This is a challenging assignment. It may take some time to achieve. But this goal and its rewards are great.

The recognition of a living God also has other implications. For example, just recently I was asked to intervene on behalf of a woman who is very ill and who will likely die soon. She needs a feeding tube at this point just to keep on going a little while longer, but her doctor was reluctant to provide it for her since her prognosis is so poor. But as someone who believes in a living God and in the God who resides within every holy human life, I suggested that this patient be given nutrition. And she has responded remarkably well to it. This does not mean that she is cured, but as I have often said, even when a cure is not possible, healing is always possible. This woman is now alert, awake and able to converse with members of her family who have flown in from all over the country to be with her. Perhaps she will even have the opportunity to bless her family, just as Jacob blessed his children before he died.

God is central to everything that happens in the Book of Ruth. His living presence enables Boaz and Ruth to make appropriate choices when they are all alone at night on the threshing-floor. Their restraint demonstrates that human behavior can be molded in different directions. Earlier in history, right after receiving the

Torah, the Israelites could not resist the temptation of building and worshipping a Golden Calf. Earlier still, Eve could not resist the temptation of the forbidden fruit. But one night, alone on a threshing-floor, Ruth and Boaz demonstrate that anything is possible, and their behavior leads to redemption. Such redemption can come only when we have assimilated the concept of a living God within ourselves. Only then can we demonstrate who we really are.

Chapter 13

WHO ARE YOU?

One of life's fundamental questions – "Who are you?" – appears at two significant points in our story. The first instance occurs when Ruth uncovers the feet of Boaz: *"And it was at midnight, that the man was startled and [he] turned about – and behold – there was a woman lying at his feet. And he said, 'Who are you?' "* [1]

There are so many ways to answer that seemingly simple question. We can respond with our name, gender, age, occupation, citizenship, marital status, or by using many other identifiers that seem appropriate in any given situation. Yet what are we really trying to convey? And do any of our responses get to the essence of who we really are as individuals?

The Book of Ruth goes out of its way to explore the question of identity, both internal and perceived. The text presents this question – "Who are you?" – twice within the same chapter, catching our attention and forcing us to think about this most significant issue. While the question appears in two different contexts and is asked by two different people, only one person – Ruth – provides the answer.

---

[1] Ruth 3:8–9

Boaz is the first to ask her, as we have seen. And when Ruth returns to Naomi's home very early the following morning, having spent the night away, Naomi greets her with words similar to those Boaz used: *"Mi at biti?" – "Who are you, my daughter?"* [2]

So much is contained in those few words. Naomi is saying: "I know I told you to behave in this special way, but are you all right? Has your status changed? Are you married or engaged? Will he marry you? Have you had relations with Boaz? Did you exercise sexual restraint? What transpired in that field and how have you been changed and transformed by this experience?"

Naomi recognizes what many people do not: change is essential to human development. Most people would agree that new patterns of thought and behavior might lead them to a richer, fuller life, lessening their degree of pain and suffering. Yet most people don't want to have to *change* in order to achieve these ends! They do not take advantage of second chances. They find a certain comfort and security in repeating the same old patterns, even when these hold them back.

Strange as it may seem, prisoners and slaves find reassurance in their daily routines, and sometimes choose a life of oppression over unknown freedoms. Think of the Israelites who suffered such cruelty as slaves to the Pharaoh in Egypt. Yet after being liberated by Moses, every time they faced risk or uncertainty, they cried out that they wanted to return to bondage. They forgot all the bad and remembered only the good. No sooner did they cross

---

[2] Ruth 3:16

the Sea of Reeds that they longingly reminisced about the pots of meat and bread they used to eat in Egypt.[3]

But change is necessary for personal growth. Life is a process of continuous change and transformation. If you always stay the same, it may be convenient, but are you alive? Or rather, are you just existing? And if you are the same at age 40 as at 20, woe unto you. If people recognize you all the time, it may even mean that you are boring. So it seems strange that some people think that being asked, "Who are you?" implies a negative judgment. While one may change for the worse, having a dear friend or relative exclaim, "Who are you? I don't recognize you!" can be a great compliment.

People need to take risks in order to grow, just as Ruth did in following Naomi's directives. Ruth risked her life and her reputation. She could have been attacked by the robbers from whom Boaz was protecting his property. And Boaz, upon being awakened so suddenly, might have feared he was being attacked. He could have struck Ruth, injuring or killing her. Even if he had recognized her right away, they might not have exhibited sexual restraint.

When Naomi asks Ruth *"Mi at?"* she wants to know exactly what happened. She also wants to know if Ruth was able to maintain her equilibrium and function as her best self in extraordinary circumstances. She soon finds out that everything turned out well, perhaps even better than she had hoped for.

---

[3] Exodus 16:3

Two contemporary examples come to mind in which such risk-taking allowed people to grow and develop:

I first met Sylvia about fifteen years ago. She was a young, highly successful woman who seemingly had it all. A corporate attorney, she was married with two children. But as she disclosed to me, all her life she had been sexually frigid. The more that she explored her own psyche, the more insight she found into the causes of her frigidity. At the onset of her puberty, her mother had unknowingly frightened her about her body and her sexuality. Rather than describing menstruation as an anticipated passage into womanhood, Sylvia's mother focused on how Sylvia would now need "protection" – from men in general. "Trust me; don't trust men," her mother told her. Sylvia also came to realize that at the core of her being, she was fearful. Unconsciously, she had always been afraid that every sexual act could be experienced as a form of violation and rape.

Fortunately for Sylvia, she recognized and acted on her second chance, her opportunity to change old patterns. She found the courage and inner resources to transform herself, becoming much more comfortable in her sexual relationship with her husband. She was able to be more open about her own sexual desires and fantasies, and she even began to take the initiative at times. When her husband came home late one night, he found her wearing provocative new lingerie. He was pleased but surprised, and as he swept her into his arms, he whispered playfully, "Who are you, gorgeous?"

Marlene's story is quite different, but in another sense, the same. She was in her mid-thirties, married and a homemaker with one child, a kind woman with a profound lack of self-worth. As she told her story, it became apparent that she had suffered unwitting abuse at the hands of her mother throughout her life. Her mother was a driven, narcissistic individual, whose every thought and deed revolved around herself. Marlene was the youngest of three children. She was always passive and compliant. She found it very hard to stand up to anyone, including her mother. But through counseling, she slowly learned how to assert her independence of mind and spirit. One day, when Marlene finally found the courage to answer her mother in a tone and with words she had never before used, her mother yelled, "Who are you?" She answered, "I will tell you who I am. I am Marlene. I am a person. I am a wife. I am a mother. I am a sister. I am also your daughter. And I serve God in the best way I know how."

What Marlene expressed so simply, yet so beautifully, was a reality that is usually the core issue in everyone's life. Marlene had come to recognize a living God in her life, and this allowed her to grow, progress and develop her potential. She gained the courage to change and to explore new relationships with family and friends. This process involved more than discovering psychological insights. Marlene actually underwent profound spiritual transformation.

Each of us can similarly transform ourselves as we journey through life. The Book of Ruth, and the entire Torah, provide the road map for this process, especially for the times when we are given a second chance to mend old hurts, correct old wrongs, or change old patterns.

Chapter 14

RESPONDING TO PAIN

We might regard the story of Ruth as something unique, the story of one special individual and her family. Yet, on closer inspection, we find that the Book of Ruth contains many ideas that we have come across before. In fact, the Book of Ruth basically contains the essential lessons of the entire Torah. Through Ruth, we come to understand that all we really need is the example of one individual. The Torah is not meant to be understood only on an esoteric, philosophical level. It also constitutes a practical guide for how to live our daily lives, particularly in our relationships with those who are closest to us. It guides each of us, as individuals, in interacting kindly with every other individual, particularly those in our families.

Some may find it easier to be kind than others. But one thing is certain: Most of us find it far easier to be kind to strangers than to those closest to us. A physician, mental health care worker or other healer spends a limited amount of time with a patient or client. Rules of professionalism, politeness and propriety are easy to observe.

But in the bosom of the family, among the people with whom we are closest in the world, acting kindly is a far greater challenge.

How can we learn to behave at our best with those who are around us throughout the day, not just for 15 or 50 minutes? How can we express our true identities – our lights and our shadows – without hurting those nearest and dearest to us?

The story of Ruth shows us that such behavior *is* possible, *is* achievable. For the Book of Ruth describes how a relationship with a living God leads to the greatest acts of kindness that take place within the family.

Achieving such a living relationship and performing acts of kindness, particularly within our families, are goals that are open to everyone. The *process* of achieving these goals relates to recognizing and responding to the essence of the human condition. When life events happen which are destructive and painful, we first need to acknowledge our own pain. Then, we may be able to recognize the similar circumstances and similar pain of others. At that point, our compassion for what others are experiencing can be awakened. And ultimately, we can learn to act proactively, with kindness, to ease the pain of others, and in the process, our own pain as well.

Each of us learns this lesson in a different way. I think of Teresa, one of the finest, kindest nurses I have ever met. She spends her days caring for the sickest of the sick, including many with communicable diseases. Without hesitation, she dons a gown, mask and gloves and enters the rooms of those whose conditions are highly contagious. Some of her patients have skin lesions that are unsightly, open sores that are painful to look at, let alone treat. But in all of her visits, Teresa remains caring, optimistic and encouraging. Many of her patients rightly regard her as a ministering angel.

But Teresa is human after all, as she recently commented to me. She is married to a fine man who puts in long days at his law firm. Normally, even though Teresa is exhausted at the end of her shift, she and her husband dine together and find time to listen to each other's stories and concerns. They both feel that this special hour helps bring balance to their lives and their relationship. But maintaining that balance is challenging.

"You wouldn't have recognized me if you heard me last night," Teresa told me recently. "I'd just come home after eight hours, and all I wanted was a hot bath and a chance to relax. Alex walked in the door and before I could even greet him properly, he started to tell me that he was not feeling well. He told me that he felt a cold coming on, that he ached and had chills. He headed for the most comfortable chair in the den, propped his feet up, and asked me to bring him a hot cup of tea. Well, I just kind of snapped. I don't know exactly what words I used, but they were not particularly well-chosen. And I really yelled. I think I called him a 'childish bastard.' My patients wouldn't have believed that I was capable of relating to anyone like that, certainly not a family member."

Teresa's behavior was perfectly "human." However, the Book of Ruth teaches us how we might better respond to such challenges. Our mission is to show kindness not only in our professional lives, but also in our private lives, including at the end of the day when we are tired. After all, the way that we relate to our family members indicates who we really are when we remove our masks. The only other time we reveal ourselves in such an intimate way is in our relationship with God. Such intimate moments present special challenges, yet special rewards.

Whenever we greet someone, it is important to remember that all of us have been shaped by our experiences. Life is not easy, as we all know. It is inevitably filled with pain, struggle and hardship. People respond to the pain in their lives in different ways, some of them destructive to themselves and to others.

Different ways of responding to pain may be seen by comparing the Book of Ruth with the Book of Job. Both books deal with great human suffering and loss. The losses described in each are quite similar. However, the *responses* to suffering are strikingly and remarkably different.

Both Job and Naomi lose their possessions and children, without any reasonable hope of perpetuating their family names and lineages. They each complain about how their lives have become bitter, although they realize that God is present in all that occurs to them. Job says, *"As God lives... Who has embittered my soul."* [1] Naomi says, *"The Almighty has embittered my soul greatly."* [2]

Both Job and Naomi suffer to such an extent that their external appearances are changed. We read about Job's friends that, *"They lifted up their eyes from afar and they did not recognize him, and they raised their voices and wept."* [3] And when Naomi returns from Moab

---

[1] Job 27:2

[2] Ruth 1:20

[3] Job 2:12

to Bethlehem, we are told that, *"The whole city was astir at their arrival, and they said: 'Is this Naomi?' "* [4]

Despite the terrible difficulties and calamities that both Job and Naomi face, each of their stories is resolved happily. Job has more children and Naomi, who has treated Ruth as a daughter, not a daughter-in-law, is blessed with a grandson who is even called her son.

But how is the happy ending achieved in each book? Throughout the story of Job, he and his friends engage in philosophical discussions about the nature of the world and man's place in it. Their discussions do not lead to any emotional resolution or kindness. Job concludes that he has limited human perspective and must recognize the ultimate infinite wisdom of God.

By contrast, in the story of Ruth, although God does not appear to act directly at all, the kindnesses of Naomi, Ruth and Boaz become Divine manifestations. The people in the story, performing their many acts of *chesed*, loving-kindness, help bring about the building of the house of King David.

They thus make it clear that acts of *chesed* can help resolve difficulties. Kindness has great power, so much so that it can even affect God. As the *Midrash* teaches, "Boaz did what he had to do, and Ruth did what she must do, and Naomi did what she was supposed to do. God said also: 'I shall do My part.' "[5]

---

[4] Ruth 1:19

[5] *Midrash Ruth Rabbah* 7:7

Furthermore, as we have already discussed, practicing kindness within the family is the most challenging, yet most important goal for each of us. Such constant and consistent ways of relating to family members represent the true meaning of love.

Part IV: LOVE AND REDEMPTION

The Book of Ruth (Summary of Chapter 4)

Boaz goes to the gate of the city, where he encounters Tov, also known as Ploni Almoni, Ruth's other potential marriage partner and redeemer. Boaz speaks to the man in the presence of ten elders of the city, asking him if he is willing to redeem Elimelech's land by buying it from Naomi. The kinsman says yes. Boaz then reminds the kinsman that he will have the related responsibility of marrying Ruth since, "On the day you acquire the field from Naomi, and from Ruth, the Moabitess, wife of the deceased, you will have acquired it in order to perpetuate the name of the deceased upon his inheritance." At this point, the kinsman changes his mind, allowing Boaz to purchase the land and marry Ruth in a transaction witnessed by the people. The people then bless Boaz and Ruth, linking them to the Matriarchs Rachel and Leah. Boaz and Ruth marry and a son is born to them. Naomi helps Ruth raise the baby, and the women neighbors say, "A son has been born to Naomi." These women name the baby boy Oved. He will become the father of Jesse, the father of King David. The last five verses of this chapter, which conclude the Book of Ruth, present the genealogy from Peretz to King David.

Chapter 15

THE OTHER MAN, THE OTHER WOMAN
AND MARRIAGE

"Boaz had gone up to the gate and was sitting there, and behold, the [other] redeemer was passing by – [the one] of whom Boaz had spoken...." [1]

People are complex. Nowhere do we see that more clearly than in interpersonal relationships, particularly between men and women. Western culture promotes the romantic notion of falling in love and finding one's true love or soul mate. In literature, song and film, two strangers spot each other from across a crowded room and realize that they are destined for one another. And such moments and events actually *do* occur in real life, but we are told only part of the story. We read about or view the external reality, without knowing all of the complexities that lie beneath the surface.

Relationships cannot be summed up as neat little packages involving two people. There are always other issues and people involved. And that makes perfect sense, because each soul is complex, made up of many parts. While part of one's soul can

---

[1] Ruth 4:1

connect deeply with another human being, other parts of the soul remain isolated and alone. As the great Danish writer Jens Peter Jacobsen observed:

> It was the great sadness that a soul is always alone. Any belief in the merging of one soul with another is a lie. Not the mother who took you onto her lap, not a friend, not the wife who rested next to your heart....[2]

Furthermore, no two people exist as a unit in a vacuum. In every relationship there is bound to be "another man" or "another woman."

One very happily married man was brave enough to share a personal story that illustrates just this point. One recent evening, his wife told him that she was bothered by her thoughts and fantasies. She loved her husband a lot, she assured him, but from time to time memories of other people she had dated came to her unexpectedly. She could not understand why she was still thinking about other men at this fulfilled, happy time of her life. Her husband, a wise and compassionate man, was perceptive and understanding enough to respond in a most thoughtful manner: "You're a human being," he told her. "Of course you have thoughts like that. That is normal and natural. It doesn't change the loving relationship that we share." While this man's intention was to illustrate the reality of "the other person" in a relationship,

---

[2] Jacobsen, J.P. *Niels Lyhne.* Translated from Danish by Tiina Nunnally. Seattle: Fjord Press, 1990, p. 203. Originally published in 1880.

he actually revealed something more – the beauty of his own marriage. His wife trusted him enough to share a deep, inner part of her soul, and he was wise enough to understand and to respond in a way that made both of them feel comfortable, understood and even more loved.

In the Book of Ruth, the "other man," another potential suitor for Ruth, who has a closer relationship (an uncle) to her than does Boaz (a cousin), makes his appearance in the last chapter of the book, chapter 4. He is described in a most remarkable way: *"Boaz had gone up to the gate and was sitting there, and behold, the [other] redeemer was passing by – [the one] of whom Boaz had spoken – and he said [to him], 'Come over, sit down here, So-and-so,' and he came over and sat down."* [3]

The English translation cannot fully do justice to the term that is used in Hebrew, *Ploni Almoni,* translated as So-and-so, i.e., John Doe. Rashi explains this term based on its Aramaic translation, meaning "concealed and secret." Rashi's understanding is in perfect harmony with what Jungian psychology calls the "shadow," the dark part of the Self and the unconscious that is always there.

In the story of Ruth, *Ploni Almoni* has a name that is identified in the *Midrash,* Tov, meaning "good." [4] The *Midrash* tells us that Tov is actually Elimelech's brother, and therefore Boaz's uncle. [5] He is thus related more closely to Ruth than is Boaz, and he has

---

[3] Ruth 4:1

[4] Ruth 3:13

[5] Rashi, Ruth 3:12

the first right – privilege and obligation – to redeem and marry her and acquire her property. Tov's name gives us an immediate clue as to his nature, for often when a person is known outwardly as "good" – someone who projects an image of one polished or refined – his or her shadow is even larger than most. Beware of a person named Good. A person named Good might say, "I have all the time in the world for you," but when you say, "How about next Monday?" he will probably say, "Sorry, I'm busy. Can we make it another time?"

Up until this point, the characters in this story have seemed too good to be true. Only Elimelech and his sons had any explicitly identified negative traits, and they met early deaths. Boaz, Ruth and Naomi appear to be righteous in every way. Now comes an encounter with someone who is less than perfect – Tov, Mr. "Good" – and the level of tension in the story rises.

Boaz convenes a court of ten men in front of whom he proposes a business deal to Tov. He sets out some very attractive elements of a legal and financial matter: *The parcel of land which belonged to our brother, Elimelech, is up for sale by Naomi who has returned from the Moabite country. And I decided to tell you about it, in these words – Buy it in the presence of those sitting here, and in the presence of the elders of my people. If you desire to redeem it, redeem it, and if it will not be redeemed, tell me, that I may know [now], for beside you there is no one to redeem it, and I am [next in line] after you."* [6]

---

[6] Ruth 4:4

Tov's response is prompt and to the point. *"I will redeem it,"* he says.[7]

But then Boaz further explains and defines the nature of this business arrangement. He reminds his relative that this is a "package deal." On the day he redeems and acquires the field from Naomi and from Ruth, the Moabitess, wife of the deceased Machlon, he will also have acquired the obligation to perpetuate the name of the deceased upon his inheritance, i.e., to marry Ruth as well.

Now Tov has a change of heart. He publicly reveals his true priorities, as well as his ignorance of the law. He remembers quite rightly that male Moabites are barred from converting to Judaism (based on their ancestors' not offering bread and water to the Israelites during their wanderings in the Sinai desert). Such an ethic is diametrically opposed to the teachings and personal example of Abraham, the father of the Jewish people, who rushed to greet visitors and supply them with food and shelter.

Perhaps Tov does not know that *only* Moabite males may not convert to Judaism, as the women of Moab played no part in the tribe's thoughtless, inhospitable behavior towards the Israelites. Perhaps he does not know, or perhaps he is aware that others are not well-versed in this aspect of Jewish Law and that a great deal of prejudice against Moabites (whether men or women) exists amongst his neighbors. Perhaps he is unduly concerned about his status and reputation. Perhaps he was willing when only a business arrangement was involved, but when an emotional aspect –

---

[7] Ruth 4:4

marriage to Ruth – enters the picture, he changes his mind. Whatever his reasons, he immediately reconsiders his response to Boaz: *"I am unable to redeem it for myself, for I would mar my own inheritance; redeem it for yourself and assume my right of redemption, for I am unable to redeem it."* [8]

Overshadowing his thoughts is the notion that if he enters into a marriage with Ruth, there will forever be a blemish on his own children. I wish I could say that things have changed a great deal in the thousands of years that have passed since the time of Boaz and Tov. But you know as well as I do that most people remain overly concerned about any blemish – real or perceived – on their names and reputations.

Furthermore, many people I meet and know are like *Ploni Almoni* in another way. They are perfectly willing and capable of entering into business arrangements. They may be excellent providers who carry out every detail of their financial and legal obligations for their families. Yet the one thing they cannot do is provide for someone *emotionally*; they cannot enter into a meaningful *relationship* with another human being.

Mrs. Thompson sat in my office one afternoon describing her husband, a successful accountant: "Everyone thinks that George is terrific, and of course he is in many ways. He's certainly brilliant and talented. He's an excellent provider and knows how to keep things running smoothly, despite his busy schedule. He's got our computer programmed to help remind us of appointments, lessons, payments due and everything else you can imagine. Some

---

[8] Ruth 4:6

of our payments are deducted automatically from our checking account so I don't have to worry about them. And this guy, who has so much on his mind, remembers to take out the trash as he goes out the door each morning. Sounds perfect, doesn't he?"

But Mrs. Thompson went on to explain that her wonderful husband was also emotionally withdrawn and unreachable. She could never communicate with him about the things that really mattered in her life, in their life together. Their marriage "deal" included everything but a true soulful relationship. Such was the situation with *Ploni Almoni*, who was willing to help financially as long as his heart was not part of the deal.

Boaz's response is completely different from that of *Ploni Almoni*. His actions emphasize the spiritual legacy of the marriage union. Near the dramatic conclusion of the book, Boaz publicly carries out a complex transaction: *"Boaz then said to the elders and to all the people: 'You are witnesses this day that I have acquired all that belonged to Elimelech, and to [his sons], Kilyon and Machlon, from the hand of Naomi. And moreover, Ruth, the Moabitess, the wife of Machlon, I have taken as a wife, to perpetuate the name of the deceased upon his inheritance, that the name of the deceased be not cut off from among his brethren….'"* [9]

By taking Ruth, the wife of Machlon, as his wife, Boaz will perpetuate the name of the deceased. He is directing his energy and attention to this historic second chance – to the future, not the past. He hopes to have a child with Ruth, who will continue not only the family line, but also the Israelites' spiritual legacy.

---

[9] Ruth 4:9–10

The verses that follow seem to emphasize this point even further: *"Then all the people who were at the gate, and the elders, said: 'We are witnesses! May God make the woman who is coming into your house like Rachel and like Leah, both of whom built up the House of Israel....' "* [10]

The people who witness this ceremony at the gate of the city, along with the elders (i.e., the court that Boaz has convened), bless this union, praying that God will bless Ruth who is coming into Boaz's home, making her *"like Rachel and like Leah, who together built the House of Israel."* [11] This is an amazing statement. This court is comparing Ruth, a Moabitess convert, to the great Matriarchs of Israel!

The implications of this utterance are remarkable. Anyone reading through the Bible notes the names of the Matriarchs that are recorded there: Sarah, Rebekah, Rachel and Leah. And that list seems to be firmly established, fixed and unchanging. Yet here, in the Book of Ruth, we see that this is not the case at all. Ruth, by virtue of her special abilities, attributes and qualities, is added to the list of Matriarchs. Her elevation to that status demonstrates something extremely important: *A second chance and opportunity can be used to achieve anything, even something that is seemingly fixed, closed and impossible.*

The people's prayer on behalf of Ruth continues, combining the past and the future in one seamless line. They pray for *"the*

---

[10] Ruth 4:11

[11] Ruth 4:11

offspring which God will give you from this young woman." [12] And indeed, that is the focus and culmination of this entire story. For Ruth conceives and gives birth to a son. The women surrounding Naomi tell her: *"And he will be unto you a restorer of life, and a support in your old age, for your daughter-in-law who loves you has borne him, and she is better to you than seven sons."* [13]

Oved will not only be a blessing to Ruth and to Naomi. He will also grow up to become the father of Jesse, who will beget David. And David will be more than a revered King and Psalmist. In Judaic tradition, he is the progenitor of the Messiah.

---

[12] Ruth 4:12

[13] Ruth 4:15

Chapter 16

WHAT IS LOVE? WHAT IS MOTHERHOOD?

The Book of Ruth describes almost every sort of family relationship – husband-wife, parent-child, mother-in-law-daughter-in-law, uncle-niece, uncle-nephew and cousin-cousin. Yet, strangely, throughout the many descriptions of significant moments in the lives of these people, the word "love" is absent. It appears only once in the story, near the very end, and there it describes the special relationship between Ruth and her mother-in-law, Naomi. Naomi's female friends and neighbors bless Naomi and say that her daughter-in-law loves her: *"… For your daughter-in-law who loves you has borne him…."*[1]

The depth of love between these two women, and the way in which each one demonstrates it, is truly remarkable. Early in the story, Ruth risks everything familiar and easy in her life in order to accompany, honor and assist her bereft mother-in-law. Ruth could have left. She could have abandoned Naomi and no longer been exposed to certain hardships and problems, as well as to Naomi's sadness. But Ruth cleaves to Naomi, and the two women share a difficult journey and challenging times of despair and deprivation.

---

[1] Ruth 4:15

The special bond between Naomi and Ruth is based on deep mutual trust.

I am reminded of two women I know, both survivors of the same concentration camp during World War II. Throughout their years of suffering, they saw each other's nakedness – physical, emotional and spiritual – and shared each other's food. They protected each other and looked out for one another. Having together survived those traumatic experiences, they forged a very deep bond of trust and friendship, and they feel closer than sisters. They truly love one another.

This same unshakable love is what Naomi and Ruth shared and what Boaz and Ruth shared. The love between Boaz and Ruth is not described in romantic terms, but rather in terms of their total commitment to each other and to a life of kindness. The elements of kindness, commitment and love are inextricably linked. For example, the prophet Jeremiah describes God's love for His people, Israel, in these words: *"I remember in your favor, the devotion [chesed] of your youth, your love as a bride, when you did go after me in the wilderness, in a land that was not sown...."* [2]

Similarly, Ruth cleaved to Naomi and followed her along a difficult journey to a new land. Rising above one's immediate, personal needs is the essence of kindness and commitment. So is focusing on each person as an individual. Naomi did not judge Ruth harshly because she was the daughter of Eglon, king of Moab. She was not concerned with the social standing of her

---

[2] Jeremiah 2:2

daughter-in-law. It is this elevated level of relating to others that helps to bring about the era of the Messiah and redemption.

As we have seen time and time again, acts of kindness predominate in the Book of Ruth, while romantic love does not. To better understand the distinction between romantic love and kindness, I turn once again to my favorite author, Jens Peter Jacobsen. In his great work, *Niels Lyhne*,[3] his title character, Niels, reflects on romantic love:

> …[E]very palace of happiness that rises up has sand mixed into the foundation on which it rests, and the sand collects and runs out beneath the walls, slowly perhaps, imperceptibly perhaps, but it keeps running, grain after grain…. And love? Love is no rock either, no matter how much we want to believe it is.[4]

As Jacobsen so astutely observes, romantic love is fragile and fleeting. By contrast, when Boaz decides to marry Ruth, his decision is not based on the passion of the moment. After all, Ruth is not Boaz's first love. He has already been married and is now a widower, and a recent one at that. But now, when an opportunity arises for a meaningful new relationship, Boaz responds with love and kindness. Lasting love is built upon a foundation of kindness, a series of selfless acts that are meant to benefit the recipient, rather than oneself. For example, a husband

---

[3] Jacobsen, Jens Peter. *Niels Lyhne*.

[4] *Ibid.*, p. 143.

with no interest in jewelry might rush out to buy his wife a gift of this sort because it will please her and meet her needs. It will make *her* feel prettier.

Now, near the end of the story, Ruth's boundless love enables her to share her most precious possession with Naomi – her newborn son, Oved. This is no ordinary child. His birth, which is quite miraculous, is the first birth recorded in the Book of Ruth. Ruth and her first husband, Machlon, bore no children, and neither did Orpah and Kilyon. Yet, after ten years of barrenness as the wife of Machlon, Ruth conceives from Boaz, her 80-year-old husband, on their wedding night.

The passage that describes the birth of a son to Ruth, and the reaction of those around her, yields fascinating clues about the importance of this occasion: *"And so, Boaz took Ruth and she became his wife; and he came to her. God let her conceive, and she bore a son. And the women said to Naomi, 'Blessed be God who has not left you without a redeemer today! May his name be famous in Israel. He will become your life-restorer, and sustain your old age; for your daughter-in-law, who loves you, has borne him, and she is better to you than seven sons.'"* [5]

As we see, Ruth did not merely conceive. *"God let her conceive,"* illustrating the miraculous nature of the infant's conception on his parents' wedding night. And this baby will be a "life-restorer," *meshiv nefesh*, to Naomi. This Hebrew phrase is quite beautiful, literally meaning a "soul restorer."

---

[5] Ruth 4:13–15

So we are to understand that up until this point in our story, while Naomi has been acting with extraordinary kindness, sensitivity and delicacy towards every person in her life, she has also felt a gnawing soullessness. She has lost her husband and sons, losses that might have caused others to become despondent, despairing and bitter. Yet Naomi has been kind, even in her embittered condition. She has helped bring about Boaz's redemption of and marriage to Ruth. Naomi plays a pivotal role in this narrative.

The child is not merely Naomi's grandson – the women refer to him as Naomi's son: *"Naomi took the child, and held it in her bosom, and she became his nurse. The neighborhood women gave him a name, saying: 'A son is born to Naomi.' "* [6]

Naomi imbues this child with spiritual nurturance, transmitting to him her ethics, values, kindness and love. No one can receive too much love. It may not take a village to raise a child, but the more loving, caring adults who transmit lasting values to him, the better. But how does Ruth feel about this? This is her first-born (and only) son and yet she is being asked to share the honor and role of motherhood with Naomi. Ruth possesses a special quality that allows her to understand this, as well as the other moments in her life. She understands that an important role has been assigned to her – to "build up the House of Israel" like Rachel and like Leah, the Matriarchs.

---

[6] Ruth 4:16–17

The blessing of the people at the gate[7] allows Ruth to understand her life from a *transpersonal* perspective. She now sees that by responding to a historic chance, she has become part of a chain, fulfilling a much greater role.

To experience life in a narrow, *personal* way is to lead a very limited and painful existence. If "me" and "mine" are one's central concerns, then anything unpleasant that happens to the self will induce feelings of loss, devastation and suffering. Yet most people do lead their lives from this perspective, resulting in lifetimes filled with unbearable, quiet despair.

From a transpersonal perspective, however, all is possible and all is bearable. One begins to see oneself as part of humanity, as part of the universal, as part of the world. It takes hard work, faith and spiritual ascendancy to reach the heights of the transpersonal. But the rewards are great.

Perhaps Naomi's female neighbors appreciate this when they name the child Oved, describing one who will literally "serve" God all the days of his life. Indeed, this is the highest aspiration that anyone can have. At the conclusion of the Torah, the life of Moses, the greatest prophet and law-giver, is summarized as follows: *"So Moses died there, the servant [eved] of the Lord...."*[8] Oved is also destined for greatness. He will beget Jesse, who will beget David, King of Israel and progenitor of the Messiah.

Ruth recognizes that she is playing a small part in the great Divine plan. She knows that the earth, and all that is in it, are the

---

[7] Ruth 4:11

[8] Deuteronomy 34:5

Lord's, and we are merely passing through a particular time and space. We each have a unique role to play, and while we are playing it, we may not even recognize its significance or importance. Ruth realizes that understanding the world in these terms is the only way to achieve happiness and, indeed, the only way to survive meaningfully.

Ruth may recall that Rachel and Leah also did not have easy lives. After many years of infertility, Rachel gave birth to only two sons, and then she died in childbirth. Leah suffered as a less-loved wife of Jacob, so that even bearing many children did not bring her immediate happiness. Yet both of these women are regarded as role models for the generations to follow. I believe that Rachel and Leah, like Ruth, managed to survive their own personal crises and challenges by focusing on something larger than and beyond themselves. They were privileged to bring into existence the sons who would establish the Twelve Tribes of Israel. Being links in this great chain and this great tradition enabled Rachel and Leah to transcend their own personal difficulties.

It is clear that Ruth is a worthy successor to these great women and that she, too, deserves to be considered a Matriarch. For she does not regard herself merely as the wife of Boaz or the mother of Oved. She understands that she has a unique opportunity to contribute to the future destiny of her people and of humankind.

Like the other Matriarchs, she is not only a mother to a biological child; she is also the Mother of Royalty.[9]

---

[9] Talmud, *Bava Batra* 91b

Chapter 17

FROM GENERATION TO GENERATION

"These are the generations of Peretz: Peretz begot Hetzron; and Hetzron begot Ram, and Ram begot Aminadav; and Aminadav begot Nachshon, and Nachshon begot Salmah; and Salmon begot Boaz...." [1]

I recently began my weekly Torah class by asking my students if their parents had ever spoken to them in a way that revealed their inner lives and allowed them to discover who they really were. Had they shared their challenges as well as their virtues? Not surprisingly, most in attendance responded that they had grown up not knowing the essences of those who sired and raised them. Their parents were highly selective in what they chose to talk about and which subjects they chose to ignore. Human sexuality was clearly in the latter category. In all cases, parents had intentionally set out to conceal from their children the parts of themselves that most embarrassed them.

This pattern is the norm, and it is certainly understandable. Parents feel burdened and threatened with an awesomely responsible role, their own expectations and those of society, as well as the cultural norms of their community. But there is pain

---

[1] Ruth 4:18–21

when parents do not speak in an honest way with their children. A void, a gap, results. The more one knows about one's past, the easier one's path through life will be. And the truth of the matter is that even when things are not said overtly to children, they usually pick up on them anyway. Furthermore, concealment only exacerbates problems, because when difficulties are put into words, voiced and discussed with others, they become more manageable and less frightening to everyone involved.

Yet, most parents continue to shy away from meaningful dialogue with their children. However, that is not the only way that they communicate with their offspring. As Clarissa Pinkola Estes describes in her wonderful study on women,[2] there is wisdom of the mind, the heart and the "ovaries." Ovarian learning applies to both men and women; it is simply another way of describing intuition.

Intuition and other forms of non-verbal communication play most significant roles in our lives, and not only in our relationships with our parents. D.H. Lawrence referred to the "whispering of the walls," the hushed echoes of past behaviors and conversations that continue to infuse themselves into our lives long after the owners of the voices have died.

From the time we are very young, we imbibe unspoken lessons about ourselves, others and the world along with our mother's milk. What we see, feel, hear and sense in other ways help shape our own worldview, our own reality. Much of this process is

---

[2] Estes, Clarissa Pinkola. *Women Who Run with the Wolves*. NY: Ballantine, 1992, p. 114.

conducted unconsciously, some of it even in *utero*. Many physicians have come to understand the importance of exposing a developing fetus to a calm, stress-free environment, one permeated by music and other soothing stimuli.

The lessons we learn from the womb on continue to have a powerful effect on us throughout our lives, in both positive and negative ways. After all, no one is born with a map or directional guide for how to navigate the world. And no one sits down and explains the strivings, challenges and unbelievable burdens of the human condition. It is so much easier to take what we have learned from those around us, consciously and unconsciously, and repeat those same patterns for ourselves. Children who are abused tend to become abusers. Sons and daughters of alcoholics often fight their own battles with drinking and other forms of substance abuse.

How remarkable, then, is the story of Ruth and Boaz, in showing us that the past need not necessarily predict what will happen in the future. On the contrary, repair of unhealthy and unwise patterns is always possible. More than that, breaking out of destructive patterns is the way to reach redemption, on both a personal and communal level.

Each year, as we sit down to the Passover Seder and retell the story of the Exodus, we talk about our distant ancestors. We acknowledge having been slaves. Ideally, we are to examine our lives at this point and discover in which ways and to which masters we are still subservient. Tracing the path of Jewish history even further back than Egypt, we read about some of our other ancestors. It is significant that we do not begin with Abraham, the first Jew. Rather, we start our story with Terach, Abraham's father, who was an idol worshipper. And it was Terach whose son Haran begat Lot, the very same Lot whose incestuous union with his eldest daughter produced Moab.

As Ruth and Boaz interact, the question becomes: Will each of them revert to the family patterns of the past, those that they have learned or absorbed? The answer is: They do not. Ruth and Boaz each behave with the utmost propriety and sexual restraint, and by doing so they correct the past. Later generations can repair the mistakes of their forebears and thereby do *teshuvah* – return to God in repentance – for them. Just as intuition can span generations, so can the process of repair, of *teshuvah*.

The Book of Ruth concludes with straightforward genealogical facts. It is unusual for a story to end rather than begin in this way. Why, then, does the Book of Ruth conclude in this manner? The point seems to be that no matter where we have come from, we each share the same ancestry. We all come from a Lot or a Tamar in some fashion. Their stories are not unique, but universal. We all experience the human condition; none of us is pure-blooded. Sometimes after a relative has died, we learn more about our family than we ever knew before. We discover additional roots and branches, some of which fill us with pride and others which do not.

But no matter. We can always begin again and choose a new path and a new pattern of behavior. The consequences of responding appropriately to a second chance are profound. For when Ruth and Boaz set off in a new direction and rectify their pasts, great things happen. These are summarized in the concluding verses of the Book of Ruth: *"And Salmon begot Boaz, and Boaz begot Oved; and Oved begot Jesse; and Jesse begot David."* [3]

It is the House of David that will usher in the era of redemption for all humankind. By virtue of the new approaches to life and to relationships undertaken by Ruth and Boaz as they break the patterns of their pasts, a hopeful future is ensured not only for their own family, but for the entire world.

---

[3] Ruth 4:21–22

Conclusion

LESSONS FROM RUTH

Chapter 18

JOURNEYS OF INDIVIDUATION

Each of us is given the opportunity to try new approaches to life, just as Ruth and Boaz did. Each of us is called upon to proceed along our own unique journey.

As we have already noted, both Abraham and Ruth undertake journeys that involve their very essences. They literally take a "leap of faith." Abraham becomes the first convert to Judaism, while Ruth follows in his footsteps many generations later, converting and building a home that will eventually culminate with the Messiah. Both Abraham and Ruth leave a home, a religion, a culture and a community to go to a place that they have never seen before. It takes the utmost belief, courage and determination to undertake such a journey and to continue on it in the face of tremendous obstacles, including the anxiety that often accompanies taking new steps in an unfamiliar direction.

As we grow, mature and internalize the values and beliefs that will guide us, we are called upon to separate – psychically and physically – from our parents as we traverse the road to adulthood, thus becoming our own person. This process of individuation, as challenging as it may be to get to a "new land," is the first great theme of the Book of Ruth and of the entire Torah.

As we strive to individuate, we try to find out who we really are. We need to develop our own identities. In that process, we constantly encounter new situations and are often called upon to make moral and ethical decisions based on who we have become.

Will we be consistent in applying the principles that guide us or will temptations sometimes get the better of us? How will we respond to the question, *"Who are you?"*[1]

And so the second great theme of the Book of Ruth, and of the entire Bible, concerns acquiring our own identity, knowing who we really are, and letting others know who we are. The only thing that can give us the strength to live life in this way is the knowledge that God is always with us. That promise is explicitly made to Jacob in the Book of Genesis: *"And behold, I am with you, and will keep you wherever you go… for I will not leave you."* [2] This is the only knowledge of which we can be certain, the only fact that can comfort us when we are feeling utterly alone and abandoned.

As we have seen, God infuses the lives and worldviews of everyone in the story of Ruth. Boaz even greets the harvesters in his field by saying, *"God be with you,"* and they respond, *"God bless you."* [3] Furthermore, they act in God-like ways. When Boaz promises Ruth, *"I am a redeemer,"* [4] he indicates that he will act as Ruth's protector and shelter her from harm – that he is a man of God.

And how does Boaz or anyone else come to recognize the presence of God? One needs to create a bridge between regular, "ordinary" life – every seemingly mundane activity – and Divinity,

---

[1] Ruth 3:9; Ruth 3:16

[2] Genesis 28:15

[3] Ruth 2:4

[4] Ruth 3:12

and to recognize that God's message is timeless, eternal and applicable to all circumstances.

Acceptance of Divine laws and practices represents the highest level of faith. It is equivalent to setting forth on a journey to a new land that one has never before seen. Such is the journey towards conversion, undertaken first by Abraham, later by all of the Israelites at Mount Sinai, and later still, by Ruth.

The history of the Jewish people is based on conversion. The Bible makes clear that from the beginning, converts played pivotal roles in the development of the Jewish people. Once again, we see a parallel message in the Torah and in the Book of Ruth. In Exodus, we are reminded that Moses, the greatest leader of his people, married a woman who converted to Judaism. She was Tzippora, the daughter of Jethro, a *"priest of Midian."*[5] Just as Tzippora came from a distinguished background, so did Ruth.[6] Both of these women came from the elite classes of foreign cultures, where they worshipped foreign gods. Yet Tzippora helped Moses bring about the Israelites' redemption from slavery in Egypt, and Ruth and Boaz will bring about the redemption of all of humankind.

At the outset of this book, we talked about trying to understand why the lineage of the Messiah is what it is – why it emanates from the troubled pasts of Ruth and Boaz's ancestors. As we have examined the lives of Boaz and Ruth and their families, perhaps we have come to see that their experiences are

---

[5] Exodus 2:16

[6] Rashi, Ruth 1:2

representative of *all* human pain and suffering. Their lives epitomize the human condition. It is vital that the Messiah, who is to usher in an era of redemption, emanate from such universal human circumstances. His lineage also forces us to look at our own lives in a different way, examining dark corners that we may have chosen to ignore or to hide for years, perhaps generations. Furthermore, this story teaches us that the Messiah will arise from a place where people will not be looking for him. He will be a person who no one expects to fulfill this pivotal role in the history of humankind.

The Book of Ruth also teaches us how we are to look at and interact with the nations around us. We are to recognize our commonalities and shared origins. We are to welcome converts and rejoice in greeting anyone who wants to join us in striving to be a light unto the nations. Our individual and collective journeys, if they are guided by acts of kindness, will enrich ourselves and the world as – together – we try to find our way back to God.

Chapter 19

A LIVING GOD

The Book of Ruth is read publicly on Shavuot, the festival commemorating the Israelites' acceptance of the Torah at Mount Sinai.

In explaining why, the *Midrash* [1] states: "Why is the Book of Ruth read on the festival, at the time of the giving of the Torah? It is because this Scroll is entirely *chesed* [loving-kindness] and the Torah is entirely *chesed*...."

The centrality of loving-kindness in the Torah is similarly discussed in the Talmud.[2] Rabbi Simlai states that, "the Torah begins with *chesed* and ends with *chesed*. It begins with *chesed*, as it states, '*And the Lord God made for Adam and for his wife garments of skins and clothed them*,'[3] and ends with *chesed*, as it states, '*And He [God] buried him [Moses] in the valley....*' "[4]

Rabbi Zeira makes a similar point:[5] "This Scroll [of Ruth] deals with neither ritual uncleanliness nor cleanliness, with neither prohibitions nor what is permitted. So why was it written? To teach you how great is the reward for those who carry out acts of loving-kindness."

---

[1] *Midrash Lekach Tov*

[2] *Sotah* 14a

[3] Genesis 3:21

[4] Deuteronomy 34:6

[5] *Midrash Ruth Rabbah* 20:15

God Himself is the role model for such kindness. He introduces His giving of the Ten Commandments and the entire Torah with a statement of His great kindness in redeeming the Israelites from slavery in Egypt: *"I am the Lord your God who brought you out of the land of Egypt, out of the house of bondage."* [6]

Kindness certainly seems quite commendable. We have all been taught that it is a great virtue. But there is something more to be learned from these rabbinical discussions and Biblical citations. Notice *when* some of these acts of kindness, particularly Divine kindness, take place. It is *after* someone has sinned. God clothes Adam and Eve *after* they have eaten from the fruit of the forbidden tree, even *after* they have transgressed the first prohibition given to humankind. And God buries Moses *after* he has struck the rock twice to bring forth water, thus violating God's commandment in full view of the entire nation. [7]

So the most important lesson of the Book of Ruth is not just to be kind, but to show kindness in particular to those who have gone astray – something you can only do if you have a living God. Acting kindly, with the experience of a living God in your heart and soul, transforms you and allows you to usher in the next phase for the coming of the Messiah.

---

[6] Exodus 20:2

[7] Numbers 20:11–12

APPENDIX A

The Family Genealogy
The Origins of Ruth

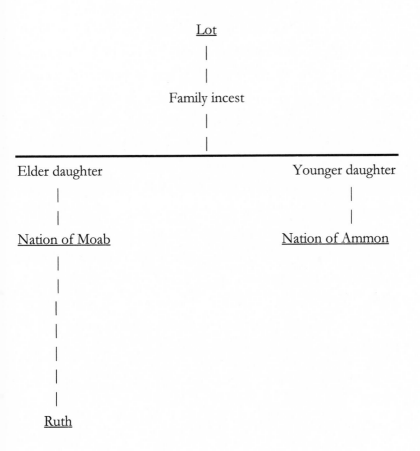

APPENDIX B

The Family Genealogy
The Origins of Boaz

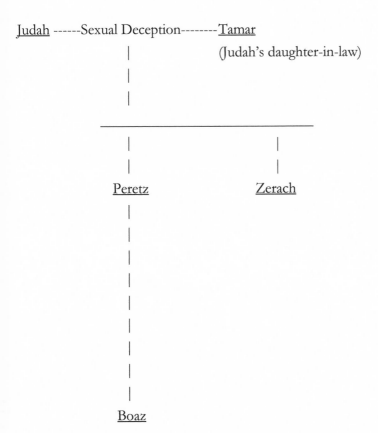

Judah ------Sexual Deception--------Tamar

(Judah's daughter-in-law)

Peretz   Zerach

Boaz

APPENDIX C

The Family Genealogy
The Origins of Royalty

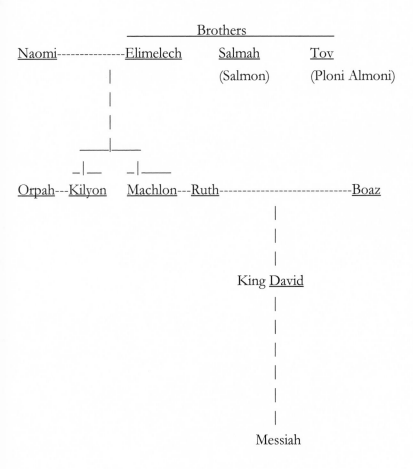

APPENDIX D

The Family Genealogy – A Note

The year is 1800 BCE. Fire rains on Sodom and Gomorrah. The twin cities that epitomize the worst of human cruelty and depravity are destroyed by God. From the wreckage flee four survivors – Lot (the nephew of Abraham), his wife and his two daughters. But Lot's wife does not make the journey; she turns to gaze backwards in longing and is thus preserved in salt. Lot and his daughters flee to a cave. His daughters mourn the destruction of the world as they know it. This is the end of the earth, this is the end of humanity, they wail. But hope in second chances springs eternal, and they hatch a plan – to intoxicate their father, seduce him and repopulate the earth. From this incest, two boys are born, Moab and Ben-Ami, and they give rise to the nations of Moab and Ammon.

* * *

Fast forward 300 years. Judah, the son of Jacob, has not fared well. His eldest son married a beautiful woman named Tamar, and then he died. His second son, according to the custom of the time, took Tamar as his wife, but then he also died. Judah must also marry off his third son to Tamar, but he doesn't want to. Beautiful Tamar languishes, waiting to become a wife, as well as a mother of a child from the tribe of Judah. Her hope wanes, but refusing to believe she has no more chances left, she takes matters into her own hands. She disguises herself as a prostitute and deceives and seduces Judah himself. Judah does not learn of what she has done until it is discovered that she is pregnant. She gives birth to twin boys, Peretz and Zerach.

* * *

Fast forward another 600 years. A widow named Naomi is returning home to the Land of Israel from self-imposed exile. That exile has been most unhappy for Naomi – she lost her husband and her two sons. Her only comfort is her daughter-in-law, Ruth – a Moabitess, a descendant of Lot's daughter's union with her father – who has refused to abandon her in her time of trial. Upon her return, Naomi devises a successful plan to marry Ruth to the elderly but kindly judge, Boaz, who happens to be a descendant of Judah's son Peretz.

About the Author

Rabbi Levi Meier, Ph.D., is Jewish Chaplain of Cedars-Sinai Medical Center in Los Angeles. He is a licensed clinical psychologist and a marriage, family and child therapist. He has authored numerous books on spirituality and psychology, including *Ancient Secrets: Using the Stories of the Bible to Improve Our Everyday Lives*, which has already been translated into Hebrew, German and Italian.